THE PLAN OF CHICAGO

CHICAGO VISIONS AND REVISIONS

A series edited by
Carlo Rotella, Bill Savage, Carl Smith, *and* Robert B. Stepto

Also in the series:

Barrio: Photographs from Chicago's Pilsen and Little Village
Paul D'Amato

The Plan of Chicago

Daniel Burnham and the Remaking of the American City

CARL SMITH

THE UNIVERSITY OF CHICAGO PRESS

CHICAGO & LONDON

The University of Chicago Press, Chicago 60637
The University of Chicago Press, Ltd., London
© 2006 by Carl Smith
All rights reserved. Published 2006
Paperback edition 2007
Printed in the United States of America

19 18 17 16 15 14 13 12   9 10 11 12 13

ISBN-13: 978-0-226-76471-9 (cloth)
ISBN-13: 978-0-226-76472-6 (paper)
ISBN-10: 0-226-76471-0 (cloth)
ISBN-10: 0-226-76472-9 (paper)

Library of Congress Cataloging-in-Publication Data
Smith, Carl S.
The Plan of Chicago: Daniel Burnham and the remaking of the American city /
Carl Smith.
p. cm. — (Chicago visions and revisions)
Includes bibliographical references and index.
ISBN 0-226-76471-0
1. Burnham, Daniel Hudson, 1846–1912. 2. City planning—Illinois—Chicago—
History—20th century. I. Title. II. Series.
NA737.B85S65 2006
711'.40977311—dc22
2006005125

To

THE ART INSTITUTE OF CHICAGO,

THE CHICAGO HISTORY MUSEUM,

THE NEWBERRY LIBRARY,

and

NORTHWESTERN UNIVERSITY
ACADEMIC TECHNOLOGIES

CONTENTS

List of Illustrations ix

Acknowledgments xiii *Introduction* xv

1. Planning Before the Plan 1

2. Antecedents and Inspirations 11

3. The City the Planners Saw 34

4. The Plan Comes Together 54

5. Creating the Plan 71

6. Reading the Plan 86

7. Promotion 111

8. Implementation 130

9. Heritage 151

Bibliographical Essay 169

Index 175

ILLUSTRATIONS

1   Chicago's strategic location   3

2   The "Burnt District" after the Great Fire of 1871   4

3   Raising the city's grade   6

4   The transformation of Paris   13

5   The model town of Pullman   16

6   Hull-House complex   17

7   First Regiment Armory   18

8   Map of the World's Columbian Exposition   20–21

9   The Court of Honor at the World's Columbian Exposition   22

10 Olmsted Brothers' proposal for Grant Park   27

11 Draft of Burnham speech to the South Park Commission   28

12 Burnham's 1904 design for the lakefront   30

13 Traffic at Dearborn and Randolph streets, 1909   37

14 Marshfield Avenue Station   40

15 1904 downtown transportation map   41

16 Gerard & Rabe Clothing Manufacturers   44

17 Striking messenger boys, 1902   45

18 Back of the Yards alley   46

19 Chicago Historical Society   47

20 Newberry Library   48

21 Art Institute of Chicago   49

22 Popular amusements   50

23 The Coliseum   51

24 Daniel Burnham, ca. 1910 55
25 Rookery Building 58
26 Burnham and Root 59
27 Burnham's cabin at the world's fair 60
28 Burnham and associates at the fair site 61
29 Railway Exchange Building 63
30 Planners meeting in Burnham's office 73
31 Estimate of costs 75
32 Edward H. Bennett 79
33 Jules Guerin 84
34 *Plan of Chicago* 88
35 Opening illustration from the *Plan of Chicago* 89
36 *Plan of Chicago* title page 90
37 View looking west over the city 92–93
38 A uniform cityscape 96–97
39 Proposed arrangement of streets 100
40 Elevation of the Civic Center 104–5
41 Holograph page from first chapter of Burnham's draft 108
42 Holograph page from first chapter of Burnham's draft 109
43 "Are you foolish enough to do it?" 115
44 Charles H. Wacker 118
45 Lantern slide of the Civic Center 120–21
46 Lantern slide of downtown traffic 123

47 Bond rally 124
48 "Chicago Children Study Big City Betterment Plan" 126
49 Burnham grave 127
50 Michigan Avenue before widening 135
51 Michigan Avenue Bridge and Michigan Avenue 136
52 Michigan Avenue Bridge at the river 137
53 Circle Interchange 138
54 Chicago River during straightening 140
55 Construction of Municipal Pier 142
56 Navy Pier, ca. 1920–21 143
57 Grant Park, 1929 144
58 North Lakeshore Drive in the 1880s 145
59 Extension of the Outer Drive, 1955 146
60 Homage to Bennett in Millennium Park 149
61 Construction of Congress Expressway 152
62 Lakefront cultural institutions 153
63 Bird's-eye view of the Century of Progress International
     Exposition on Northerly Island, ca. 1933 155
64 Dedication of O'Hare passenger terminal 156
65 Proposed Michigan Boulevard 158
66 Proposed plaza west of the new Field Museum 160–61
67 Harold Washington Library Center under construction 163
68 *Chicago Metropolis 2020* 166

ACKNOWLEDGMENTS

This book is a revision of the version that appeared in 2005 in the electronic edition of the *Encyclopedia of Chicago*. I am deeply grateful to the Art Institute of Chicago, the Chicago History Museum (formerly known as the Chicago Historical Society and referred to as such throughout this book), the Newberry Library, and Northwestern University Academic Technologies for making both versions possible. I am especially fortunate to have had the opportunity to work with the remarkable people and research resources of these institutions and organizations. This volume's dedication is a small but deeply felt recognition of what my long association with them has meant personally as well as professionally.

Numerous people deserve special recognition for all their help in the selection of the contents and preparation of the text. The knowledge and skill of Sarah Marcus, Chicago Historical Society project director for the *Electronic Encyclopedia of Chicago,* were indispensable in providing access to essential materials, as was research specialist Lesley Martin's extraordinary grasp of the richness of CHS's magnificent collections. Rob Medina, the society's rights and reproduction coordinator, was very supportive in providing images, and Gwen Ihnat expertly reviewed the original text. James R. Grossman, the Newberry Library's vice president for research and education and co-editor of the *Encyclopedia of Chicago,* suggested many valuable editorial improvements, as did the two anonymous readers for the University of Chicago Press. Northwestern University students Sarah Ansari, Sherri Berger, Kathryn Burns-Howard, Jenna Carls, Kimberly Kocek, Andrew Kurland, Abigail Masory, Courtney Podraza, Kathryn Schumaker, and Milena Zasadzien provided exceptional research assistance.

The generous role of the Art Institute of Chicago was coordinated by Ryerson and Burnham archivist Mary Woolever. Harlan Wallach and Stefani Foster, both of Northwestern Academic Technologies, took the photographs of contemporary Chicago and of the cover of the *Plan* that are included in the illustrations, and they played critical roles in the creation of the original electronic version. Warm thanks are also due to R. Russell Maylone, curator of the Charles Deering McCormick Library of Special Collections in the Northwestern University Library, and Wilmont Vickrey, founding principal of VOA Associates. Chicago Historical Society executive vice president and chief historian Russell Lewis, Northwestern Academic Technologies director Robert Taylor, and Art Institute of Chicago director of libraries Jack Perry Brown supervised the efforts of their respective institutions.

I am very grateful to Professor Janice L. Reiff of the University of California at Los Angeles for suggesting this project in the first place, and to her *Encyclopedia of Chicago* co-editors, Professor Ann Durkin Keating of North Central College and James R. Grossman, for their continuing encouragement. Professor Brian M. Dennis of Northwestern was a splendid colleague at every stage. I wish to thank Robert P. Devens of the University of Chicago Press for proposing this book and for the many things he did to make it a reality, and senior manuscript editor Erin DeWitt for her excellent work in editing the book manuscript. I very much appreciate that my fellow editors of the Press's Chicago Visions and Revisions series—Carlo Rotella of Boston College, Bill Savage of Northwestern, and Robert B. Stepto of Yale University—were enthusiastic in wishing to include it in our list. As always, Jane S. Smith provided essential moral and intellectual support from start to finish.

INTRODUCTION

The *Plan of Chicago* of 1909, more familiarly known as the Burnham Plan—after its principal author, architect and city planner Daniel H. Burnham—is one of the most fascinating and significant documents in the history of urban planning. Its fascination arises from the imaginative and visual appeal of its stirring prose and stunning illustrations, which combine to persuade the reader of the merit of its ideas. Burnham and his collaborators in the Commercial Club of Chicago, whose membership consisted of the city's leading businessmen, contended beyond any uncertainty that boisterous Chicago required major alterations and that the creation of a finer city was within reach. The *Plan's* significance rests in the fact that it helped convince so many people at the time and since, including some of its critics, of the truth of this contention.

While the *Plan* exemplifies the enduring aspiration of elite members of urban societies to make their cities grander and better organized, it also reflects the circumstances of a particular historical moment. The nineteenth century was the age of urbanization and industrialization, especially in the United States and western Europe. Between 1800 and 1900, the proportion of the American population living in urban areas (defined modestly in the federal census as places with 2,500 or more residents) ascended dizzily from just over 3 to almost 40 percent (the total population meanwhile went from 5,308,483 to 76,212,168). The country's leading city, New York, exploded in this period from 60,515 to 3,437,202 (or over 4.5 percent of the entire nation), and by 1900 there were thirty-eight places with more than one hundred thousand residents. America's most remarkable urban phenomenon, however, was Chicago. In 1830 it was a tiny settlement of perhaps one hundred people. A decade later it had 4,470 inhabitants, making Chicago the ninety-second biggest city in the country. By 1890 the number was 1,099,850, and it had moved up ninety places. By 1910, the year after the *Plan of Chicago* was published, the count was 2,185,283.

It is hard to appreciate in retrospect how provisional and rough-edged turn-of-the-century Chicago remained, despite the fact that its economic and social base, as well as many of its physical features, were well established. While it could (and certainly did) boast of numerous impressive cultural institutions and its recent triumph with the World's Columbian Exposition of 1893, Chicago was still an unruly place. Much of the cityscape was filthy and ugly, smoke pollution and faulty sanitation were unpleasant and unhealthy hazards, freight and passenger movement through the downtown was slow and inconvenient, a wide swath of railroad tracks isolated much of the city south of the river (including its commercial center) from the lakefront, and many streets were unpaved. A large number of working people lived amid marginal and sometimes desperate circumstances, so that eruptions of class antagonism and labor violence, though always unwelcome, were rarely unexpected. Astonished by the city, the fair, and the contrasts within and between them, the historian and cultural analyst Henry Adams famously observed, "Chicago asked in 1893 for the first time the question whether the American people knew where they were driving."

The *Plan of Chicago* tried to answer this question, at least as far as cities were concerned. In so doing, it takes its place alongside other contemporary attempts to understand and improve Chicago. To name just two examples, Upton Sinclair's *The Jungle* appeared only three years before the *Plan,* Jane Addams's *Twenty Years at Hull-House* the year after. While their assessments of Chicago and their recommendations for reforming it were strikingly different from the *Plan,* the authors of all three books were confronting a similar group of concerns. Was it possible not only to determine the direction of urban experience, but also to make a major correction? More specifically, could cities be transformed into more orderly, beautiful, and humane settings without stifling the energies that propelled them? Might economic interests, the public good, and personal needs be reconciled? And could Chicago even become not just equal but superior to any other great city of the world, past or present?

The *Plan of Chicago*'s answer to all of these questions is a self-assured yes. Its ambitious proposals and its peremptory confidence in them are characteristic of the belief of civic-minded businessmen during the Progressive era in the necessity of redeeming American cities and their ability to accomplish this through rational reform. The *Plan* would not have been possible without the aggressive participation of the Commercial Club, whose vision of Chicago it unapologetically conveys, but the club would not have undertaken this project and the *Plan* certainly would not have anything like its prominence and authority without the full force of Daniel Burnham's experience, wisdom, imagination, vigor, resolve, and charisma. The *Plan* discloses, however, the Commercial Club's and Burnham's blind spots as well as their insights, their conservatism as well as their grasp of modernity, their personal presumption as well as their faith in their city. Here, too, the *Plan of Chicago* is a reflection of its times and its origins, which no individuals, no matter how forward-looking, can transcend.

CHAPTER ONE

PLANNING BEFORE THE PLAN

The *Plan of Chicago* establishes its authoritative tone and announces its ruling assumptions in its opening pages. Urbanization, the *Plan* declares, is a defining condition of modernity. The current growth of cities was unprecedented, as was the increase in wealth and the advance of democracy. But "the formless growth of the city," which had produced overcrowding and congestion, was "neither economical nor satisfactory." As a result, the *Plan* explains, "practical men of affairs are turning their attention to working out the means whereby the city may be made an efficient instrument for providing all its people with the best possible conditions of living." As for Chicago, its sudden emergence as a major metropolis was merely a prelude to its seizing its rightful place as the preeminent city of America and the world. It could only attain that position, however, if it exercised the vision and will required to discipline and direct the powerful but disparate physical and social energies that, having created this prodigious city, now threatened its undoing. Chicago's spectacular development had resulted in "the chaos incident to rapid growth, and especially to the influx of people of many nationalities without common traditions or habits of life."

Chicago emerged so abruptly, the *Plan* explains two chapters later, that events outran its citizens' capacity to comprehend and control them. Over the seventy-five years—a single human lifetime—in which this outpost with only a smattering of settlers exploded into a great metropolis encompassing close to two hundred square miles and more than 2 million residents, the city's expansion was "so rapid that it has been impossible to plan for the economical disposition of the great influx of people, surging like a human tide to spread itself wherever opportunity for profitable labor offered place." The public interest now demanded that Chicagoans lift their eyes from their limited personal concerns to those of the fundamental structure and organization of the built urban environment in which they all lived. A coherent and compelling strategy for creating a "well-ordered and convenient city" was now nothing short of "indispensable." These words, like many other passages in the *Plan of Chicago,* have inspired readers since they were published on July 4, 1909. The choice of date was noteworthy, for the *Plan* was a declaration of independence from what its framers saw as a self-imposed tyranny of unregulated development that threatened the fortunes, and perhaps even the lives and sacred honor, of the city's citizens.

But was it true that Chicago had evolved without any plan? In fact, by 1909 it had been the site of many plans. While the city always attracted opportunists focused only on immediate gain, as early as the 1830s it was being fashioned by people who consistently looked ahead. This hardly means that they did not often pursue very short-term—and shortsighted—goals. But they consistently and actively attempted to create what was by their lights a better city, in the belief, shared by the authors of the *Plan,* that improving Chicago as a whole would benefit everyone who lived within it.

The place and the times rewarded Chicagoans' efforts to grow their own and their city's fortunes. Modern Chicago owes its origins to its location at the southwestern edge of the Great Lakes near a convenient portage to the Mississippi Valley and the heart of the continent. The most distinctive feature of the setting was, paradoxically, its lack of distinctive features. The level prairie that stretched in all directions away from the lake invited the most ambitious conceptions by offering few obvious natural obstacles to their realization. The prairie and the lake, the *Plan* observes, "each immeasurable by the senses," dictated the scale of possibility in Chicago. "Whatever man undertakes here," it continues, "should be either actually or

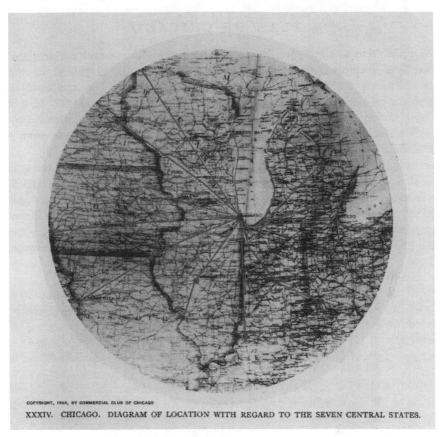

COPYRIGHT, 1909, BY COMMERCIAL CLUB OF CHICAGO

XXXIV. CHICAGO. DIAGRAM OF LOCATION WITH REGARD TO THE SEVEN CENTRAL STATES.

FIGURE 1.   This map appears on the first page of chapter 3 of the *Plan of Chicago*. It demonstrates Chicago's "location with regard to the seven central states"—that is, Ohio, Indiana, Michigan, Missouri, Iowa, Minnesota, and Wisconsin, not to mention the rest of Illinois. The radiating lines, colored in red in the *Plan,* emphasize how well connected Chicago was to smaller cities in the region. Chicago Historical Society (ICHi-39070_3e).

seemingly without limit." While European explorers recognized the area's promise as early as the 1670s, the fulfillment of its potential had to wait for the right historical moment. This arrived in the antebellum decades with the onset of the industrial, transportation, and communications revolutions in the United States.

These developments animated an increasingly networked national and international free-market economy, a jump in both immigration

FIGURE 2.   This is the third of several editions of this map of the devastation caused by the
Great Chicago Fire of 1871 that were published by the R.P. Studley Company of St. Louis,
with proceeds going to the victims of the fire. There were many different versions of this
map. In this one, north is to the right. The fire's point of origin, behind the Near West Side
cottage of Catherine and Patrick O'Leary, is located at the upper left-hand point. The map
dramatically displays not only the extent of the destruction but also how the fire leaped the
South and Main branches of the Chicago River as it moved north and east, destroying the
downtown and most of the North Side. Chicago Historical Society (ICHi-14894).

from abroad and population mobility within the nation, and an ethos
of hyperbolic boosterism, the local form of the national rhetoric of
manifest destiny. Chicago was home to nearly thirty thousand people
by 1850 and to ten times that number only twenty years later. After the
Great Fire of 1871 incinerated close to a third of the city, including
the commercial downtown and most of the North Side, Chicago was
speedily rebuilt, thanks to the irrepressible spirit of local residents and
an infusion of capital from investors elsewhere who knew the country needed this great central marketplace. None of this happened
smoothly. Considerable tumult, whether in the form of financial busts
that alternated unpredictably with the booms or social and economic
tensions that all too often erupted into violence, marked the city's
growth through the late nineteenth and early twentieth centuries.

Where was planning in all of this, or did the invisible hand of
market forces take care of everything? In a noted address delivered in

1923 at the Field Museum to the Geographical Society of Chicago and appropriately titled "Chicago: A City of Destiny," J. Paul Goode, professor of geography at the University of Chicago, argued that the advantages of the city's location, and the local population's ability to understand and exploit these advantages, made Chicago's eminence inevitable. Thirty-two years later, Harold M. Mayer, another University of Chicago geography professor speaking under the same auspices, complicated Goode's argument. Mayer began his lecture, "Chicago: City of Decisions," by citing five deliberate actions that "have carried [Chicago] toward its destiny as the Metropolis of the Midwest." These included the provision of the federal Land Ordinance of 1785 that dictated Chicago's (and many other towns') rectangular street grid, the building of Fort Dearborn near the mouth of the Chicago River in 1803, and the choice by railroads to make Chicago what historian William Cronon has called the "gateway city" between the industrializing East and the agricultural hinterland. Of interest here is that Mayer's other two examples were the creation of the *Plan of Chicago* and "the decision to set up planning as a continuous operation in Chicago."

Mayer stated that he picked these five decisions "more or less arbitrarily." He claimed that he could have chosen any of a number of other examples. Among them were many of the developments he and his coauthor Richard C. Wade later described in *Chicago: Growth of a Metropolis* (1969). These included the cut in the sandbar that had impeded entrance to the Chicago River and the construction of a harbor at that entrance, both accomplished by 1833; the expulsion of the Native American population shortly after; the greatly anticipated and much-delayed completion of the Illinois and Michigan Canal, which was finally in operation by 1848; the raising of the city's grade and the construction of a comprehensive waterworks, both of which began in the 1850s; the establishment of the South, West, and Lincoln parks and the boulevard system that connected them, starting in the late 1860s; and the successful reversal of the flow of the Chicago River, after several earlier attempts, during the 1890s. All of these entailed planning in that they were long-term coordinated efforts usually involving direct or indirect public participation, approval, and financing. Chicago was also the site of several large-scale privately funded planning initiatives, among them the opening of the Union Stock Yard in 1865, the building of the model town of Pullman in the 1880s, and the creation of the Central Manufacturing District in 1905. As the *Plan* said of its own purpose, the aim of all of these was "to anticipate the needs of the future as well as to provide for the necessities of the present."

In ways that transcend any individual example, the planning idea is deeply ingrained in the nature and character of Chicago. The city's lack of a long history, at least from the point of view of those not of Native American ancestry, both invited and demanded planning. One of the things that distinguished Chicago from the other leading American cities that, with the exception of New York, it surpassed in population by 1890 was the comparative brevity of its past. What history Chicago did possess its residents commonly ignored because they felt little connection to it. Through the nineteenth century,

FIGURE 3. Chicago's swampy and low-lying setting led to its being literally raised several feet. Some buildings were not only lifted but also moved to different locations. In this view of Lake Street in 1855, which building contractors used as an advertisement, the work goes on in the background as the cosmopolitan passersby seem to pay little mind. Edward Mendel, Chicago Historical Society (ICHi-00698).

Chicago's population consisted overwhelmingly of those who, if not from somewhere else themselves, were children of parents born and raised in other places. Commonly this elsewhere was a different and distant country. And if members of the city's commercial and social elite were largely native born, they, too, had mostly come to Chicago from other parts of the United States.

Even in the early twentieth century, when the *Plan of Chicago* appeared, self-made men constituted the bulk of this elite, though more and more the sons of such economic pioneers were taking positions of leadership. For much of the city's population, moving to Chicago and allying oneself with its future had been central to their own personal plans for success. Indeed, few places were so speculatively oriented. It is no coincidence that Chicagoans created the modern commodities market, in the form of the Chicago Board of Trade, where the future itself is bought and sold. Nor was it out of the city's character that real estate developers purchased property in sparsely settled areas in anticipation of the growth that was sure to make the investment pay.

Nowhere else in the United States did booster rhetoric rise to such brassy grandiloquence. Of the countless speeches and tracts that boomed Chicago's prospects, few outstripped the hyperbolic optimism of the thick volume *Chicago: Past, Present, Future,* subtitled *Relations to the Great Interior, and to the Continent,* first published in 1868 by John S. Wright. Wright arrived from western Massachusetts in 1832 at the age of seventeen. Before he was twenty-one, he made a fortune in real estate speculation. Wright prepared a census and one of the earliest maps of Chicago, and he constructed at his own expense the town's first public school. Wright's real estate profits evaporated in the Panic of 1837 (he lost another fortune twenty years later investing in a new kind of reaper), but his faith in the city's prospects never wavered. Well before J. Paul Goode's address to the Geographical Society, Wright contended that the natural creation had been planned with Chicago's greatness in mind. "It is clear as sunlight," he proclaims, "that for Illinois, Wisconsin, Minnesota, Iowa, North Missouri, and part of Indiana and Michigan, this city must be the emporium." Of all America's new western cities, Wright likewise declares, Chicago "is most certain to grow." Speaking of the city's nondescript topography, Wright adds, "There never was a site more perfectly adapted by nature for a great commercial and manufacturing city, than this."

One could dismiss all of this as bombast, except for the fact that it was true. In 1861 Wright reportedly predicted that within a quarter of a century the city's population would reach 1 million. He was off by only four years. Wright's main point was that, whatever the momentary setbacks, Chicago's progress was irresistible. The future, the most valuable commodity in Chicago, would be bigger and better, and it would belong to those who most fully understood the potential that lay in the factors that Goode listed and who then knew how to command Chicago's promise with the kind of decisions that Mayer described. In Chicago, Mark Twain writes in *Life on the Mississippi* (1883), "they are always rubbing the lamp, and fetching up the genii, and contriving and achieving new impossibilities." For the occasional visitor, Twain explains, Chicago was always a "novelty," since "she is never the Chicago you saw when you passed through the last time."

Well before the *Plan of Chicago* was published, there were also those who anticipated its assertion that in their haste Chicagoans had built all too carelessly and with insufficient planning. Legendary landscape architect Frederick Law Olmsted, reflecting on the Great Chicago Fire in the *Nation* shortly after the conflagration occurred, was only one of several observers who attributed the extent of the damage to hurried and sloppy building. Olmsted—who had recently designed the South Side's Jackson Park and Washington Park, as well as the elegant suburb of Riverside—would twenty years later be one of *Plan* author Daniel Burnham's chief collaborators on the World's Columbian Exposition of 1893. Chicago's "weakness for 'big things,'" its desire "to think that it was outbuilding New York," Olmsted wrote, did not directly cause but certainly invited the disaster. The editors of the *Chicago Inter-Ocean* at the time agreed, stating that the fire revealed that the city's "paramount need was harness, self-restraint, the temperance which comes from experience." None of these qualities thrived in Chicago.

At the turn of the twentieth century, numerous observers criticized the apparent governing spirit of Chicago and other cities for thinking of planning, if at all, merely as a matter of expanding the urban infrastructure in ways that would attract and support yet more private commercial investment. It was bad policy, these critics maintained, to entrust the future to real estate developers, project engineers, and most public officials, who rarely lifted their eyes from the matter right at hand. In too many instances, the highest concern of such people was how quickly and cheaply they could get a particular project done, not how long it would last or how it related to the city as a whole. Though by the 1880s Chicago was becoming famous for its architecture, the most skilled designers were responsible only for a limited number of buildings and did not pay a great deal of attention to the larger context as they worked on individual structures.

Some thoughtful Chicagoans complained that their fellow citizens measured civic achievement only in quantitative rather than qualitative terms, and rarely with anything but their own personal welfare in mind. As a result, Chicago suffered from being a place where all too many people came to work and invest rather than to live, and this showed in the city they had built. One of the city's most thoughtful and perceptive social observers was journalist and novelist Henry Blake Fuller, who was actually born and raised in the city but who never made peace with its booster ethos and imperious entrepreneurial spirit. Commenting on the built environment of Chicago in an article on the city in the *Atlantic Monthly* in 1897, Fuller noted with regret, "Possessed of a single sheet of paper, we have set down our crude, hasty, mistaken sketch upon it, and we shall have the odds decidedly against us in any attempt to work over this sketch, made on the one surface at our disposal, into the tasteful and finished picture that we may be hoping finally to produce." In Fuller's novel *With the Procession* (1895), a civic-minded group aptly named the Consolation Club meets to consider the affairs of their "vast and sudden municipality." One of its members remarks sadly, "This town of ours labors under one peculiar disadvantage: it is the only great city in the world to which all its citizens have come for the one common, avowed object of making money."

The *Plan of Chicago* combines familiar booster rhetoric with the reservations expressed by Olmsted, Fuller, and others. On the one hand, it contains passages that John S. Wright could have written, as when it flatly states, "Chicago is now facing the momentous fact that fifty years hence, when the children of to-day are at the height of their power and influence, this city will be larger than London: that is, larger than any existing city." On the other hand, it rejects the idea that the city's success could or should be evaluated in terms of numbers alone, or that the future would take care of itself. While Chicago's growth had exceeded the most optimistic projections, it was time to rethink some basic conceptions of civic success. Fortunately, the *Plan* states, "the people of Chicago have ceased to be impressed by rapid growth or the great size of the city. What they insist [on] asking now is, How are we living?" The answer to that question was not reassuring, and the only proper course of action, the *Plan* asserts, was to prove Fuller's pessimism wrong and triumphantly remake the city.

CHAPTER TWO

ANTECEDENTS AND INSPIRATIONS

The *Plan of Chicago* did not appear out of nowhere, nor did its creators claim that it did. In its second chapter, "City Planning in Ancient and Modern Times," the *Plan* acknowledges a long line of city
builders and rebuilders from antiquity to the present. It does so in
part to educate its readers, but mainly to lend more authority to its
ideas by placing them within a tradition of impressive precedents.
For example, the *Plan* applauds the beauty and elegance of the Athens
of Pericles, the fifth-century B.C. statesman responsible for the Acropolis. It also praises the power and glory of Rome's architecture, as well
as that city's attention to plumbing and sanitation. By linking its recommendations to such universally recognized achievements in urban
design, the *Plan* implicitly makes claims for its own distinction.

But the city that the *Plan* presents as the model of city planning
and redesign at their finest is Paris, whose elegant regularity set the
standard for civilized urbanity. Here, we are told, planning began in
earnest in the seventeenth century during the reign of Louis XIV,
whose architects laid out the "vast reaches of avenue and boulevard
which to-day are the crowning features of the most beautiful of
cities." Especially worthy of note, in the view of the *Plan of Chicago,*
is the way these architects so foresightedly constructed squares, parks,
and avenues in areas that were barely settled. "The point of interest
to us," the Chicago planners write, "is that as Paris increased in population, the city grew according to a well-devised, symmetrical, highly

developed plan." Lest readers miss the lesson, the *Plan* adds, "It is unnecessary to do more than point out the fact that a similar opportunity is open to Chicago."

The *Plan* praises Napoleon Bonaparte for respecting and continuing the planning tradition in Paris, but its real hero is Georges-Eugène Haussmann, Napoleon III's prefect of the Seine. In the *Plan*'s view, the relevance and appeal of Haussmann's work was threefold. First, his was a comprehensive effort that took an existing major city apart and put it back together. Second, his design followed high aesthetic standards while serving the functional needs of a densely populated modern commercial center. Third, he directed this design to the end of establishing a stately urban order. Beginning in the 1850s, Haussmann undertook, as the *Plan* wished to do in Chicago, "the great work of breaking through the old city, of opening it to light and air, and of making it fit to sustain the army of merchants and manufacturers which makes Paris to-day the center of a commerce as wide as civilization itself." The *Plan* characterizes Haussmann as Daniel Burnham, its principal author, wished to see himself in regard to Chicago: as a practical urban visionary of unimpeachable taste, integrity, determination, and genius. "As if by intuition," the *Plan* says of Haussmann, "he grasped the entire problem. Taking counsel neither of expediency nor of compromise, he ever sought the true and proper solution. To him Paris appeared as a highly organized unit, and he strove to create ideal conditions throughout the city."

The *Plan* then surveys what it sees as other instances of sound planning in contemporary Europe. It praises several cities, though it singles out London as a noteworthy negative example for squandering numerous opportunities to improve its built environment, beginning with its failure to entrust its future to a brilliant architect after the Great Fire of 1666 when it did not adopt Sir Christopher Wren's rebuilding plan. Turning then to the United States, the *Plan* applauds President George Washington's wisdom in appointing the French-born engineer and architect Pierre-Charles L'Enfant to design the new national capital named after the first president, and it praises L'Enfant's plan itself for offering a dignified seat of American government. The *Plan* admires, for example, how L'Enfant's mul-

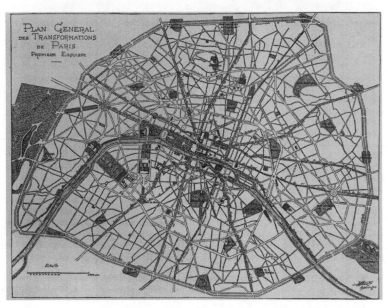

FIGURE 4. The *Plan of Chicago* includes this proposal by French architect and city planner Eugène Hénard for improving traffic patterns in Paris as an example of bold, imaginative, and comprehensive planning. Hénard worked on the Paris world's fairs of 1889 and 1900, and his ideas for moving people through the 1889 fair influenced the design of the World's Columbian Exposition in 1893. Hénard's *Études sur les transformations de Paris* appeared in installments between 1903 and 1909. Among other ideas for which he is credited are the one-directional traffic circles that many cities use at busy intersections. Examples in Chicago are scarce, with the very prominent exception of the Circle Interchange. Chicago Historical Society (ICHi-39070_2q).

tiple diagonal avenues cut through a basic rectilinear grid, creating dramatic focal points for public buildings.

As useful as it may be to understand the *Plan of Chicago* as part of a long heritage of planning, it is perhaps more revealing to try to see it in terms of its particular time and place, as a contribution to a continuing discussion of what turn-of-the-century urban America was and might be. Chicago and other cities faced the compelling question of whether the often unsightly and unsanitary commercial and industrial metropolis should and could be transformed for the better through concerted and enlightened action. The period witnessed the creation of hundreds of local and national civic associations that claimed to be dedicated to improving urban life by making it more attractive, healthy, and efficient.

Leaders and members of such organizations were generally native born and well-to-do, and some of their ideas reflected their class prejudices as well as their concerns about urban design. They felt troubled by the presence and increasing political power of working-class immigrants, though they were aware that the economic vitality of the city depended on such people. They were particularly alarmed at contemporary labor strife that seemed to threaten the stability of urban society, the most sensational examples of which were the explosion of the Haymarket bomb in 1886 and the Pullman Strike of 1894, both of which took place in Chicago.

But if the creation of some of the new independent agencies that civic "improvers" advocated revealed distrust of local government and the electorate, there was also much on the positive side. For example, the authorization by the Illinois legislature in 1889 of the Sanitary District of Chicago for the purpose of reversing the flow of the Chicago River reflected the idea—which was an article of faith in the *Plan of Chicago*—that it was essential to think regionally and not locally in dealing with urban infrastructure. The exposé of the horrific housing conditions among the immigrant poor and the call for tenement legislation in Jacob Riis's *How the Other Half Lives* (1890), though this book focused on New York, advanced a sympathetic understanding nationally that the sources of much antisocial behavior lay in the terrible conditions in which people were forced to live. For many middle- and upper-class Americans committed to improving city life, the key to effective action was enacting the Progressive agenda of reform and regulation—including reform of government and regulation of large business interests—entrusted to supposedly objective professionals.

The first major program of Progressive city planning was the so-called City Beautiful movement, in which Daniel Burnham was the central figure. Its proponents called for transforming the urban environment, as Haussmann had done in Paris, into what they believed was a more beautiful, unified, and efficient arrangement of its parts, all interconnected with handsomely landscaped streets and boulevards. Gracing this noble cityscape would be great public architecture, preferably in the neoclassical style, including if at all possible an imposing civic center. Just as a bad urban environment brought out the worst in people forced to inhabit it, a grand one that expressed the values of civilization and order would inculcate these ideals and thus elicit the best. Such a setting would also inspire a sense of community among a city's heterogeneous population. This would in turn reduce social conflict while increasing economic productivity.

City Beautiful advocates were well aware that American cities could not be mere showplaces since these urban centers were, above all, commercial entities created to serve the needs of industrial capitalism. They believed not only that it was possible for a city to be both attractive and efficient, but also that a beautiful city would function more effectively than an unappealing one. The movement did not directly address perceived social ills and inequities as such, but placed great faith in the harmonizing powers of municipal art, expressed in magnificent parks, buildings, boulevards, and public gathering places adorned with fountains and statuary. While many of those who articulated and supported City Beautiful ideas were sincere in their belief that their goal was to improve urban life, they are justifiably open to the charge that theirs was an elitist top-down approach that expressed self-interested anxieties about polyglot urban democracy and a desire to impose their own vision of an orderly metropolis on immigrants and workers in the hope of asserting social control.

In urban America generally and in Chicago particularly, other initiatives at this time attempted to address the problematic aspects of America's metropolitan future. Several of these efforts revealed the urgency with which their advocates believed that proactive measures were required. One "solution" to the "problem" of the city was to start over and build an entirely new urban community, sometimes in convenient proximity to the old, as George Pullman did in constructing Pullman in the early 1880s in Hyde Park, which was then just outside Chicago's city limits. The Pullman community included employee housing, retail establishments, a library, a theater, and even a church, as well as an enormous modern factory. While Pullman

FIGURE 5. This map and depiction of Pullman, featuring the main factory and
the town's Hotel Florence, appeared in *Harper's New Monthly Magazine* in February 1885.
The factory is located on the north side of what is now 111th Street, the town on the
south. Some of the housing built for employees is visible on the extreme right of
the drawing. Northwestern University Library.

offered several carefully considered, often ingenious, and generally
well-meaning innovations for the organization and construction
of industrial towns, the profound social, economic, and political
divisions revealed by the notorious strike of 1894 discredited such
privately owned and managed company projects as antithetical to
workers' rights and urban democracy.

Some social commentators and activists, alarmed by what they
saw as the inherently dysfunctional nature of urban life, suggested
more radical measures within the existing city. Their ideas and actions belong to the same discussion of American urban life to which
the *Plan of Chicago* contributed. The Haymarket bombing, which
took place at a labor protest rally only a few blocks from downtown
Chicago, was one of the distressing events that prompted Edward Bellamy to write his novel *Looking Backward* (1888). Bellamy's description of a utopian Boston in 2000 anticipates the City Beautiful move-

ment and the *Plan*. The immense popularity of this book reveals that Bellamy spoke to a widely felt concern. His reconstructed Boston consists of "miles of broad streets" that are "shaded by trees and lined with fine buildings." Every section of the city features "large open squares filled with trees, among which statues glistened and fountains flashed in the late afternoon sun." Public buildings of "colossal size" and "architectural grandeur" delight the eye. The physical city is an objectification of the city's social concord. Some Chicagoans took more direct steps to engage with the problems of urban life. In September 1889 Jane Addams began her life's work in the social settlement of Hull-House on the Near West Side. By the time the *Plan of Chicago* was published, the settlement had blossomed into a complex of thirteen buildings that hosted dozens of activities aimed at addressing Addams's belief, also voiced by Bellamy, that "the social organism has broken down through large districts of our great cities."

Chicagoans who looked to force rather than understanding as the "solution" to the "problem" of the modern city constructed urban institutions very different from Hull-House. A few years before the

FIGURE 6. At the time of the *Plan*, the many facilities clustered around the former home of Charles J. Hull that served as the original Hull-House settlement included residences, a kitchen and dining room, an auditorium, a coffeehouse, a women's club, a children's building, and a gymnasium. Barnes-Crosby, ca. 1905–10, Chicago Historical Society (ICHi-19288).

settlement opened, members of the Commercial Club, which would later commission Daniel Burnham and Edward Bennett to prepare the *Plan of Chicago,* successfully lobbied the federal government for a permanent garrison of federal troops to guard Chicago—and them— from "internal insurrection," a euphemism for labor and class uprisings. To facilitate this effort, they donated the land for what became Fort Sheridan, located about thirty miles north of the city. Chicago was also a participant in the movement to build within American cities what were essentially fortresses for local military units. The firm of Burnham and his partner John Wellborn Root was hired in the late 1880s to design the imposing First Regiment Armory, strategically located at Michigan Avenue and Sixteenth Street, between the city center and the posh Prairie Avenue neighborhood where several Commercial Club members lived.

FIGURE 7. The First Regiment Armory, which went by several names between its construction in 1890 (this photograph was taken the following year) and its demolition, stood on the northwest corner of Michigan Avenue and Sixteenth Street until 1968. Chicago Historical Society (ICHi-19108).

The most important antecedents and inspirations for the *Plan of Chicago,* however, were not the works of others but of Daniel Burnham himself. If the culminating act of Burnham's career as a city planner was the release of the *Plan of Chicago,* his initial triumph was the 1893 World's Columbian Exposition, from which his subsequent planning work developed. Burnham supervised the design and building of this most successful of all world's fairs. The *Plan of Chicago* calls the exposition "the beginning, in our day and in this country, of the orderly arrangement of extensive public grounds and buildings." The Columbian Exposition as a whole, and especially the vast and statue-studded exhibition halls assembled around the grand basin in the fair's Court of Honor, was a cultural milestone that established City Beautiful principles as the standard for urban design. The central principle was the careful coordination of different elements with an eye to both efficiency and aesthetic appeal. Frederick Law Olmsted's ground plan emphasized functionality as well as visual pleasure, anticipating likely pedestrian flow patterns and integrating several modes of transportation. The fair builders devoted almost as much attention to plumbing and garbage removal as they did to monumental display. Even as it championed Beaux-Arts time-honored neoclassicism as the architectural vocabulary of the City Beautiful, the exposition embraced the most modern technologies, such as electric lighting that dazzled evening visitors to the Court of Honor.

Some observers, most notably Burnham's fellow Chicago architect Louis Sullivan, saw the fair's design as a betrayal of the city's achievements in modern architecture and a capitulation to commercial interests. In his memoir, *The Autobiography of an Idea* (1926), Sullivan condemned the fair as "naked exhibitionism of charlatanry in the higher and domineering culture, enjoined with expert salesmanship of the materials of decay." In a more measured tone, the perceptive architecture critic Montgomery Schuyler praised the fair's unified design but dismissed its plaster fair buildings as a delightful illusion with little relevance to the obstreperous metropolis beyond its gates. "Arcadian architecture is one thing," Schuyler observed, "and American architecture is another."

But none could deny the exposition's importance to the several

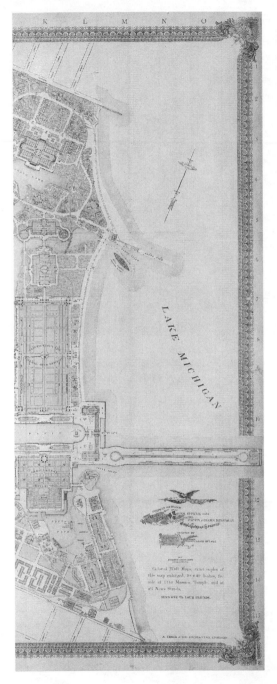

FIGURE 8. The center of the World's Columbian Exposition was the assembly of titanic buildings around the Basin in the Court of Honor, located approximately between Sixty-fourth and Sixty-sixth streets along the lake. At the north end of the fairgrounds was the Palace (or Gallery) of Fine Arts, future home of the Field Columbian Museum and now of the Museum of Science and Industry. To the west, between Fifty-ninth and Sixtieth streets, lay the attractions of the Midway Plaisance, including the first Ferris Wheel. Hermann Heinz, 1893, Chicago Historical Society (ICHi-27750).

FIGURE 9. This view is of the western end of the Court of Honor, looking southeast
across the Basin to the Agriculture Building, with Machinery Hall to the right, in front
of which is sculptor Frederick MacMonnies's Columbian Fountain. Farther east in the
Basin was the statue of the *Republic* by Daniel Chester French, who later was the sculptor
of the statue of Lincoln in the Lincoln Memorial in Washington, D.C. Charles Dudley
Arnold, 1893, Chicago Historical Society (ICHI-18013).

pioneering urban-planning projects in which Burnham participated
in the sixteen years that followed. The *Plan* cites these projects as influences, though it barely credits Burnham himself by name, perhaps
in order to appear disinterested and objective or because Burnham
did not want to seem to be immodest. The first of Burnham's city-
planning efforts involved his service—along with New York architect Charles F. McKim, Frederick Law Olmsted Jr., and sculptor
Augustus Saint-Gaudens—on the Senate Park Commission. McKim
and Saint-Gaudens, as well as Olmsted's father, had worked with
Burnham on the fair. The commission was charged with improving
the embarrassingly cluttered and shabby area of downtown Wash-

ington, D.C., west of the Capitol and south of the White House in a way that would declare the greatness of the American Republic to the nation and the world. At this point, the future site of the Lincoln Memorial (1922) was an unpromising swampy area, and Pennsylvania Railroad tracks crossed the Mall. The commission's 1901 plan is largely responsible for the arrangement of open space and monuments, cultural institutions, and government buildings as they exist today.

Almost immediately after the Washington work, Burnham was appointed by the governor of Ohio to lead a three-man team that prepared a plan to revitalize Cleveland's blighted lakefront. This plan recommended the coordinated construction of a group of large government buildings and a central railway station. The Cleveland plan of 1903 was followed the next year by a plan for San Francisco. Burnham's trusted assistant on this job was his new employee and future coauthor of the *Plan of Chicago*, thirty-year-old Edward H. Bennett, with whom he had first worked on an unsuccessful entry in a competition to redesign the United States Military Academy at West Point. The San Francisco plan proposed building diagonal boulevards that interrupted the city's orthogonal street layout, as well as other roads that followed the contours of some of San Francisco's several hills. It also called for an expansion of park and recreational space.

In spite of the fact that much of downtown San Francisco was destroyed by the earthquake and fire of 1906 shortly after Burnham and Bennett submitted their proposals, their ideas had little direct influence beyond the rebuilt city's Civic Center. Following the earthquake, many property owners, businessmen, and politicians were more eager to restore the basic layout of the pre-disaster city than to build something that seemed radically new and not immediately practical. In any event, advocates of Burnham's plan for San Francisco could not generate wide public support for its implementation. Before the work on the San Francisco plan was completed, Burnham had left Bennett in charge of the project and began another commission. This time the client was the federal government, which wanted Burnham to redesign Manila and the summer administrative capital of Baguio in the Philippines, which the United States had recently acquired in the Spanish-American War.

While all this work in other cities was essential to Daniel Burnham's continuing development as a planner, more directly pertinent to the *Plan of Chicago* were the proposals he presented in the years following the Columbian Exposition for reconfiguring Chicago's lakefront. Burnham's much-lauded triumph with the fair inspired him to design a continuous landscaped connection between the former exposition site in Jackson Park and a reconceived Grant Park (called Lake Park until 1901), the area located east of the city's center and framed by Randolph Street, Michigan Avenue, Twelfth Street (now Roosevelt Road), and the lake. Burnham was neither the only nor the first person to suggest how the downtown lakefront might be improved. Mail-order magnate A. Montgomery Ward waged a twenty-year battle, not finally resolved until 1911, to assure that the park would "remain public ground forever open, clear and free of any buildings, or other obstruction whatever," as stated on the map drawn up by the first Illinois and Michigan Canal commissioners in 1836.

For decades the chief impediment to taking full advantage of the park's location was an 1852 ordinance granting the Illinois Central Railroad the rights to a 300-foot-wide strip of land (then submerged by the lake) between Twenty-second and Randolph streets, on which the Illinois Central erected a trestle and tracks, in the process creating a breakwater that protected the shoreline from erosion. The purpose of this measure was to spare the city the expense of constructing the breakwater. The Illinois Central not only built the trestle, but also purchased from the federal government former Fort Dearborn land north of Randolph Street, where the company situated a passenger station and facilities for its rolling stock. (Former Illinois Central property between Randolph and Monroe has recently been converted into Millennium Park, which opened in 2004.)

Nineteenth-century maps and drawings reveal that much of the current parkland between the Illinois Central tracks and Michigan Avenue, as well as east of the tracks, was originally under water. It was filled in by 1890, a good deal of it shortly after the Great Chicago Fire of 1871 with rubble from the burned-out city. The lakefront was an unsightly mess, however, littered with stables, squatters' shacks, a firehouse, garbage, and debris, along with railroad tracks and service buildings. Beyond this disarray, so near and yet so far, lay the glittering lake. The city had its own hopes of redeveloping Lake Park with municipal buildings, including a new city hall. The determined Ward, at a great cost to his wallet and his popularity, won a series of lawsuits to remove current structures and prevent the erection of new ones, whether private or public. The notable exception was the Art Institute, but Ward was ultimately victorious in keeping out other proposed improvements, including an armory, a parade ground, and the Field Museum. This last institution, then called the Field Columbian Museum, was funded by Marshall Field in the wake of the Columbian Exposition and temporarily housed in the fair's Fine Arts Building, which was later substantially rebuilt as the home of the Museum of Science and Industry (1933). The new Field Museum opened in 1921 at its current site, just south of Grant Park on filled land donated by the Illinois Central.

The legal dispute over the lakefront took place in the context of a nationwide urban park and playground movement that viewed recreational space in more active terms than previously, as a place for physical exercise as well as the appreciation of nature. Reformers stressed that convenient access to parks and playgrounds was especially important for workers and their children, who endured imaginatively and physically restricted lives in the grim and endless grid. A Special Park Commission chaired by the brilliant architect and planner Dwight H. Perkins submitted a much-cited report in 1904 that bemoaned Chicago's decline between 1870 and 1900 from second to thirty-second place among large cities in the amount of park acreage per resident. It heartened the commission to discover that, thanks to the contributions of private citizens and public appropriations, the number of playgrounds in Chicago had increased from five to nine over the past four years. The commission would continue to praise such progress in its subsequent reports. Among the organizations advocating more recreational opportunities for working Chicagoans and their families was Hull-House, which built one of the first playgrounds in the city, as well as various businessmen's groups. Olmsted's sons and Burnham's architectural firm were hired to design several new parks and field houses.

As Montgomery Ward's lawsuits ground their way through the courts, Lake Park's future attracted considerable interest. Its disposition was one of the first agenda items of the Chicago Civic Federation, established in 1894 to improve the city's economic, political, and moral condition. The year after the founding of the Civic Federation, another Progressive group, the Municipal Improvement League, submitted to Mayor George B. Swift a plan for Lake Park prepared by a trio of architects, including Peter B. Wight. Wight had hired young Daniel Burnham as a draftsman for his firm in 1872. Wight's proposal revealed that he had been influenced by the example set by his one-time employee since it directly evoked the Court of Honor of the World's Columbian Exposition. The centerpiece was a pair of grand basins, north of which were a parade ground and an armory (which could double as an "amusement ground"). To the south were the Field Museum (which, it was widely assumed, would ultimately win legal approval) and a playground. The design located a new city hall and police station on the west side of the Illinois Central tracks, just north of the Art Institute and facing Michigan Avenue.

Daniel Burnham's ideas for the lakefront reflected his belief, based on his experience with the fair, in the value of thinking big. Working with his associate Charles B. Atwood, who had been responsible for the Fine Arts Building and numerous other structures at the fair, Burnham combined a new design for Lake Park with a plan to link it to Jackson Park. Encouraging Burnham was businessman James W. Ellsworth, who had been on the fair's board of directors. Ellsworth was currently head of the South Park Commission, whose authority included Jackson Park and, by 1901, the newly named Grant Park. During the spring of 1896, Burnham shared some of his ideas with Ellsworth and his fellow commissioners. In July he invited Ellsworth, several commissioners, Mayor Swift, and others to his office for a formal presentation. This was followed by more meetings and then an after-dinner speech on October 10 in Ellsworth's home. This occasion was attended by such luminaries as Marshall Field and George Pullman, and it was reported on the front page of the *Chicago Tribune* the next day.

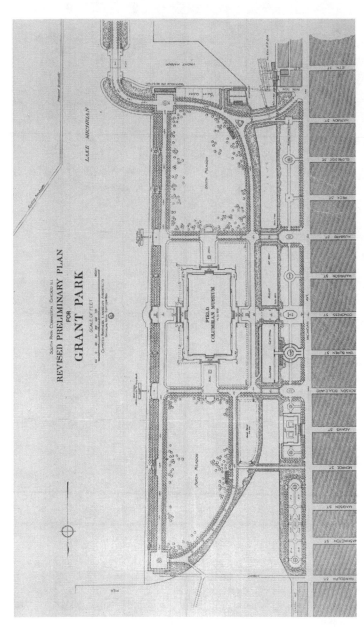

FIGURE 10. Among the many proposals for Grant Park was this one prepared by Frederick Law Olmsted's sons for the South Park Commission in 1903. The Field Columbian Museum dominates (note how much larger it is than the Art Institute of Chicago building). It is centered, as the *Plan of Chicago* would recommend, on Congress Street. North and south of the museum are large meadows, to the east are a boat landing and a lakeshore parkway bordered by trees, and to the west are the Illinois Central right-of-way, a landscaped line of basins, and then Michigan Avenue. Olmsted Brothers Landscape Architects, Chicago Historical Society (ICHi-34659).

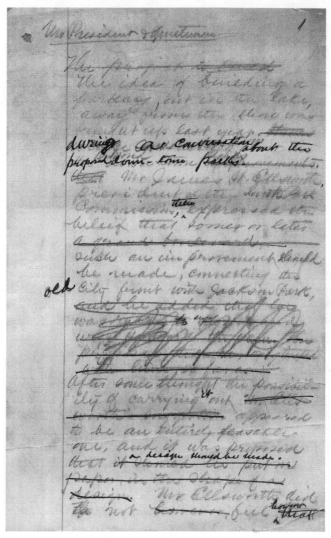

FIGURE 11. In this marked-up draft of his remarks to South Park Commission president James Ellsworth and other members of the commission on April 16, 1896, Burnham explains that the idea of building a lakeshore parkway arose the previous year during a discussion about the downtown parks with Ellsworth. "After some thought," Burnham continues, "the possibility of carrying it out appeared to be an entirely feasible one, and it was proposed that a design should be made." Daniel H. Burnham Collection, Ryerson and Burnham Archives, The Art Institute of Chicago. Reproduction © The Art Institute of Chicago.

On October 12 the paper published an editorial praising the scale of Burnham's proposals, the "taste and skill" of their conception, and the "eloquent manner" with which he advanced them. The *Tribune* also commended Burnham's "public spirit and undaunted faith in the future of Chicago." Like the fair, the *Tribune* said, this new plan demonstrated Burnham's "originality, daring, and genius," which were so aptly representative of Chicago, though the editorial ended on a more cautious note in advising that "this grand scheme involves so much work, thought, money, and originality that it should not be entered upon with haste." The city council soon passed an ordinance entrusting the lakefront and improvements to the South Park commissioners, but Ellsworth stated that nothing could be done until the state legislature authorized funding. Burnham continued to press his plan in talks before other civic organizations, among these the Commercial Club and the Merchants Club.

Burnham's design for Lake Park was a more elegant and elaborate variation on the one submitted by the Municipal Improvement League. It revealed that he believed in keeping the lakefront open and free, but not necessarily clear. Burnham dispensed with the two basins, and he shifted the park's main east-west axis a block north to Congress Street, which would extend eastward over the Illinois Central tracks and terminate in a plaza in front of the new Field Museum. Between the museum and a yacht harbor in the lake would be a great fountain. North of the Field Museum Burnham placed, as the Municipal Improvement League had also proposed, a parade ground and an armory, south of it a playground and an exposition building. One of the boldest features of Burnham's scheme was a marble-clad tunnel connecting the North and South Side lakefronts. The tunnel would begin a block north of the Art Institute, proceed under the Chicago River, and emerge on Pine Street (later North Michigan Avenue), which in turn would lead northward to Lincoln Park and, beyond that, to Evanston.

Burnham's grandest recommendation, however, was to create green space along the lake between Lake Park and Jackson Park. For the entire six-mile stretch, he stated, the city should construct new land with fill and sculpt along its eastern edge a continuous lagoon, dotted with numerous little islands and navigable by small pleasure boats. On the lake side of the lagoon would be a glorious landscaped parkway with separate paths for carriages, horseback riders, bicyclists, and pedestrians. The parkway would be conveniently linked to the mainland with numerous bridges. Everything would be arranged to offer the most advantageous views of the lake, the city, and the park itself. As for the cost, the park commissioners might produce revenue by renting land beside the new South Shore Drive to clubs, hotels, and residences.

Many of these ideas later found their way into the *Plan of Chicago,* but Burnham's approach to the lakefront looked ahead in other ways. His correspondence reveals that he understood how much the actual enactment of any proposal depended not only on its inherent merits but also on attracting and shàping public opinion. He alternately ca-joled reporters into keeping quiet about work in progress and made

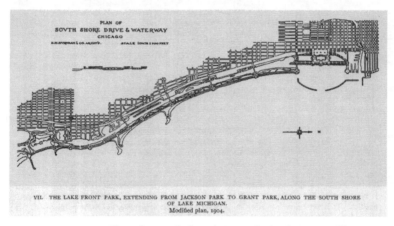

FIGURE 12.   This is the second of two drawings, the first from 1896 and this one, dated eight years later, that are reproduced in the opening chapter of the *Plan of Chicago.* They show the development of Daniel Burnham's thinking about the lakefront in the years following the World's Columbian Exposition. Both drawings proposed a landscaped lakeshore parkway and lagoon connecting a post-fair Jackson Park and Grant Park (called Lake Park until 1901). By 1904 the parkway and the lagoon were more elaborate. The design for Grant Park also changed, though the Field Columbian Museum still played a starring role. While the second plan more closely antici-pated the *Plan of Chicago,* only the 1896 design centered the museum on an extended Congress Street, as the *Plan* does. Chicago Historical Society (ICHi-39070_2d).

certain that they would attend and tell their readers about important presentations. Similarly, Burnham took care to see that potential skeptics and opponents, as well as local supporters, were invited to the presentations. He also identified the legal issues that needed attention. He used lantern slides and artists' renderings (Burnham himself executed a watercolor of the shoreline parkway) to captivate audiences, as he would in promoting the *Plan*. Lantern slides, larger and more ungainly precursors to the two-inch-square film slides that came into popular use after World War II, are a technology that dates to the Renaissance, when so-called magic lanterns were used to project images painted on glass. By the middle of the nineteenth century, it was possible to display photographic images (often colored in by hand) this way. The meticulous attention Burnham paid to even small details and his willingness to speak to multiple audiences over an extended period demonstrated both his dedication and his stamina. His promotional efforts also underscored his profound love of Chicago and his ambitions for it. He charged no fee, though his proposals and the publicity they generated were doubtless good for his architectural firm.

Burnham's speeches on his park proposals predicted some passages from the *Plan*. While he adapted these speeches to suit different audiences, they contained many similar elements, including repeated references to the lofty standard set by Pericles and Haussmann. Like all City Beautiful rhetoric, they claimed to emphasize the practical as well as the ideal—for example, the benefits planning brought to real estate values as well as to the city's civic well-being. Burnham repeatedly predicted that if Chicago became more beautiful, its wealthy residents would spend more of their money in their home city since they would no longer feel compelled to travel elsewhere to satisfy their desire to be in an aesthetically attractive place. He appealed to his listeners' faith in the greatness of Chicago and their pride of leadership, at the same time warning them that unless they acted immediately, their city would suffer and would fall behind in its competition with other urban centers. If they were concerned about costs, they should be aware that delay promised only greater expense at a later date.

That Burnham was sincere in all these beliefs is evident from his private correspondence. In February 1897 he shared his thoughts on the progress of his lakefront plans with his father-in-law and confidant John B. Sherman, who was a member of the South Park Commission for twenty-five years and succeeded James Ellsworth as its president. After explaining that his proposals were progressing nicely, Burnham made a number of characteristic statements: it was imperative to have a plan in place before proceeding with improvements; the plan must embody "the most magnificent improvement that can be desired"; the qualities he most admired in Ellsworth were his "high ideas" and willingness to "work hard for them"; and a key purpose of any improvements was to "keep our rich people and their money here, and to bring others." Two months later he wrote to Sherman again, declaring, "I am for the improvement, heart and soul. I want no money nor place, but see clearly that the best welfare of the City demands that the town should immediately put on a charming dress and thus stop our people from running away, and bring rich people here, rather than have them go elsewhere to spend their money." While Burnham frequently spoke of the importance of the lakefront to the less fortunate as well as the rich, he believed in a trickle-down approach and maintained that it was most important to develop ideas that would appeal to wealthier residents. In one 1896 talk, for example, he observed, "The more the rich spend the better for the poor."

Many passages in Burnham's speeches also expressed his visionary qualities, based on his Swedenborgian religious ideals and belief that there was a positive spirit suffusing the Creation. One of his many great gifts was his ability to move his listeners to share his view of the higher purposes of proper planning. Burnham's inspirational talents are evident in the *Plan of Chicago*. For example, the *Plan* evokes a sense of wonder when it speaks of the importance of the lake as Chicago's leading natural asset and the need for the city to take far greater advantage of its splendid presence. The lake's vast serenity, we read, induces "calm thoughts and feelings" and provides "escape from the petty things of life." It is "a living thing, delighting man's eye and refreshing his spirit." More than a decade earlier, Burnham ended some of his speeches with a similar invitation to appreciate this resource that lay waiting right at hand for all Chicagoans. "It seems," he reflected, "as if the lake has been singing to us all these years until we have become responsive and now we see the broad water ruffled by the gentle breeze upon its breast." After describing to his rapt listeners the magnificent cityscape his proposals would make possible, this most urban of men concluded, "We are merged into nature and become part of her."

CHAPTER THREE

THE CITY THE PLANNERS SAW

꧁꧂

The *Plan of Chicago* spends relatively little time discussing the Chicago that is, concentrating instead on the Chicago that might be. This is especially true of the images it contains. Of the 142 illustrations, only ten depict the city in 1909. These consist of four photographs of recreational facilities within neighborhood parks, four of major boulevards (Grand Boulevard—now Dr. Martin Luther King Jr. Drive—Drexel Boulevard, Michigan Avenue, and Lake Shore Drive), one of Grant Park, and one of Pine Street (soon to be North Michigan Avenue) looking north toward the Water Tower. All of the photographs are small and lacking in detail. The vast majority of the illustrations are either drawings of the *Plan*'s proposals or diagrams and photographs of features of European cities, most notably Paris, that the planners wished to emulate.

The *Plan* hardly ignores the actual city, however. Its creators understood that an important test of the credibility of any comprehensive proposal would be its ability to convince readers that it assessed current conditions and needs accurately. Meeting this test posed an interesting challenge for the planners, however, since they wished to affirm their confidence in Chicago's future while still contending that there were costs and even dangers in simply letting current trends continue. To put this more positively, they believed that Chicago's peerless promise justified taking bold steps—that is, measures that were expensive and potentially controversial—right away.

The *Plan* expresses this belief in its first chapter when it posits that thoughtful people agree that the age of planning was at hand. The moment was ripe to bring order out of the chaos of rapid urban growth through carefully considered systemic changes. It then observes that "the American city, and Chicago preeminently, is a center of industry and traffic." This observation is the justification of the *Plan*'s emphasis on improving commercial facilities, transportation, traffic flow, and general convenience. Since a productive urban labor force required places to play and rest, the planners also believed it was necessary to consider parks and recreational facilities. Proper design was a vital consideration in more than a narrow functional sense. A proud city, after all, like any self-respecting human being, "has a dignity to be maintained." Besides, "good order is essential to material advancement."

Two chapters later the *Plan* presents a fuller case for both Chicago's greatness and its need for planning. The city was "the metropolis of the Middle West," with economic and cultural "primacy" over a "domain" larger than Austria-Hungary, Germany, or France. Home to 2 million people, Chicago was well past its earlier period of "chance and uncertainty." Merging the rhetoric of antebellum expansion with that of contemporary reform, the *Plan* declares that it would be a betrayal of the "undaunted courage" of the resilient community that rebounded so brilliantly following the fire, "with its destiny made manifest and its wealth secure," to "fail to keep pace with the march of progress that is gathering into its ranks the progressive cities of the world." The *Plan* then proclaims, in the best booster tradition, that in fifty years Chicago would be the largest city in the world. It cites as authority the prediction of Bion J. Arnold, the respected Chicago-based engineer who served as planning consultant to numerous municipalities. Arnold had concluded "that if the national and local conditions governing the population of Chicago shall average in the future exactly as in the past," by 1952 the number of residents would reach 13.25 million. (Chicago's population did peak about that year, though at approximately 3.6 million, before dropping considerably. Slightly more than 8.7 million people lived in the entire state of Illinois in 1950. Chicago's population was about 2.9 million in 2000, an increase from slightly under 2.8 million a decade earlier.)

The rest of the *Plan*—while never failing to celebrate the city's achievements, assets, and potential—concentrates on the challenges it faced. In Chicago as in most other rapidly growing cities, there was too much ugliness and squalor. The planners blamed this condition on uncontrolled development and self-interested speculation. The *Plan* maintains that the key issue facing Chicago was no longer expansion but conservation, quality rather than quantity of life. Time and again, it declares that a city's social, cultural, and financial well-being are inseparable. "The constant struggle of civilization is to know and to attain the highest good," it states, "and the city which brings about the best conditions of life becomes the most prosperous." Lack of planning had wasted time, effort, and money, and ignoring sanitary precautions had compounded this waste by causing avoidable health problems. Parts of the infrastructure crucial to the economic vitality of Chicago—notably its streets, railroad rights-of-way, and harbor—were terribly congested, while inefficiency and disorder reigned over far too much of the city. An inescapable example of this was the helter-skelter arrangement of railroad freight yards and terminals.

Citing the work of the Special Park Commission, the *Plan* praises recent improvements but laments the paucity of parks in or near Chicago. The noise of surface and elevated cars was "excruciating," large sections of the city were filthy, and, as almost everyone at the time agreed, the level of smoke pollution was appalling. The river, which determined the city's location and remained crucial to its economy, was a disgraceful cesspool. The bridges that spanned it were inadequate, and all kinds of impediments compromised its navigability. Major streets were too narrow, and the lack of a sufficient number of diagonal roadways cutting through the grid slowed movement in any direction other than due north, south, east, or west.

Housing was also a significant problem. Too many people were forced to dwell in terrible places. "The slum exists to-day," the *Plan* explains, "because of the failure of the city to protect itself against gross evils and known perils, all of which should be corrected by the enforcement of simple principles of sanitation that are recognized to be just, equitable and necessary." Referring to recent civil eruptions, the *Plan* advances the environmentalist argument that "the frequent outbreaks against law and order" originated in "narrow and pleasureless lives." As critics have pointed out since the *Plan* first appeared, however, it spends much more time on financial rather than living and working conditions. The most intractable challenges to the city's economy, in the planners' opinion, lay not in flaws in the social order but in the configuration of the commercial downtown area bordered by the Main and South branches of the river, Lake Michigan, and Twelfth Street (now Roosevelt Road). Here, where land values (and, as a result, commercial buildings) were the highest—and where offices, stores, banks, hotels, theaters, and railroad terminals all vied for space—the city was literally choking on its own success. The overmatched streets

FIGURE 13. This image of traffic at the corner of Dearborn and Randolph streets in 1909 graphically conveys better than can any statistic how congested Chicago's downtown streets could become. Electric trolleys contend with pedestrians and with horse-drawn conveyances of multiple kinds. This photograph also documents the businesses in the Loop and the seriousness of the "smoke nuisance" at the time. Frank M. Hallenbeck, Chicago Historical Society (ICHi-04192).

were so jammed with carts, carriages, wagons, and streetcars, not to mention pedestrians, that traffic often barely budged. If the city did not act, it would not only fail to attract new business, but also current commerce would move elsewhere.

The view of the city that the *Plan of Chicago* offers was generally accurate, if clearly colored by its authors' assumptions and priorities. But gaining a reliably detailed and comprehensive understanding of turn-of-the-century Chicago was a challenge for anyone. In addition, since Chicago's physical and social features were constantly changing, an assessment might well become obsolete in the time required to formulate it. For some time, visitors' accounts had claimed that the best way to describe the city was to deem it indescribable. The young British journalist George Warrington Steevens, who came to America to cover the 1896 presidential campaign, called Chicago "queen and guttersnipe of cities, cynosure and cesspool of the world." He admitted that he could not reconcile its juxtaposition of parks and slums, "keen air" and "stench of foul smoke," and "public spirit and municipal boodle." Steevens confessed, "Not if I had a hundred tongues, every one shouting a different language in a different key, could I do justice to her splendid chaos." Writer Julian Street, who visited during a cross-country journey he undertook in order to write a book about the United States, called the city "an incomprehensible phenomenon, a prodigious paradox in which youth and maturity, brute strength and soaring spirit, are harmoniously confused." Street said that anyone trying to evoke Chicago in words would run out of adjectives and then throw a dictionary at it in frustration. "It is all that you can do, except to shoot it with statistics." Street immediately added, "And even the statistics of Chicago are not deadly, as most statistics are."

Street was right about Chicago's statistics. By 1900 Chicago occupied about 190 square miles, and, with the exception of the part of the city that now includes O'Hare Airport, it was close to its present size and shape. The largest single change in Chicago's dimensions occurred in 1889–90, when in a series of votes residents in the city and adjoining towns approved the annexation of several surrounding communities. This increased the size of Chicago almost fivefold, from less than 37 square miles to over 179. The urban infrastructure at the time the *Plan* was being prepared encompassed about 2,848 miles of streets (the longest of which, Western Avenue, extended for 22 miles) and 1,403 miles of alleys. Barely half the streets and less than a tenth of the alleys were paved. Three tunnels (at LaSalle, Van Buren, and Washington streets) and 91 city-owned and railroad company bridges went under or over the Chicago River.

In 1909, the year the *Plan* appeared, close to 38,000 streetlights, some 8,500 of which were powered by electricity (the rest were lit by gas), illuminated the city. Chicagoans talked on 208,000 telephones, eight times more than in 1900, and they consumed close to half a billion gallons of Lake Michigan water a day, 223 gallons for each resident. This required 11 pumping stations, the oldest of which was constructed at Chicago Avenue in 1854. On January 17, 1900, the Sanitary Canal had opened, fulfilling the long-standing plan of reversing the flow of the Chicago River away from the lake, thus reducing pollution of the water supply. A decade later the district opened a northern addition up to Wilmette Harbor, and shortly after that it redirected the course of the Little Calumet River from the lake and into the main canal.

Streetcars ran along the major roads in Chicago's grid, which were generally a half-mile apart, as well as on important diagonal thoroughfares. At the convergence points of streetcar lines, especially where a diagonal route met an east-west intersection, neighborhood commercial centers sprang up. Electrification of street railways began around 1890 and was close to complete by the time of the *Plan*. One could also take a cab or carriage. A one-horse vehicle charged up to two passengers fifty cents for the first mile, a two-horse carriage twice that fare. In 1910 there were just under thirteen thousand registered automobiles and some fifty reported motor vehicle deaths in Chicago. Horses pulled a host of other conveyances for personal and commercial use, and the presence of so much working livestock amid businesses and homes compounded the city's vast waste removal and sanitation needs.

The erection of rapid transit lines began in 1890. When the *Plan* appeared, four companies served the city (critics would argue it was the other way around) along elevated routes that radiated from downtown and are in large part followed by several Chicago Transit Authority lines today. The Chicago and South Side Rapid Transit Company operated its Englewood, Normal Park, Kenwood, Jackson Park, and Stock Yards branches on the South Side. The Lake Street Elevated Railway literally shadowed its namesake out to Oak Park. The Metropolitan West Side Elevated Railroad carried riders on its Garfield Park, Douglas Park, and Logan Square lines. The Northwestern Elevated Railroad's Ravenswood branch headed northwest to the Kedzie Avenue terminus. Its north-south route, which previously ended at Wilson Avenue, reached Evanston in 1908 and Wilmette four years later. In 1897 the Union Elevated Railroad constructed the now-iconic rectangular Loop, linking the various lines. By 1911 the separate rapid transit companies had merged, and by 1913 one could transfer without paying another fare.

FIGURE 14. The Marshfield Avenue Station was a major stop on the Metropolitan West Side Elevated Railroad, where it divided into its Garfield Park, Douglas Park, and Logan Square branches. The station opened in 1895 and was torn down to make way for the Congress (now the Eisenhower) Expressway. Courtesy of Janice L. Reiff.

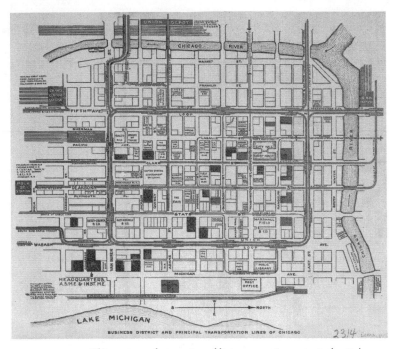

FIGURE 15. This 1904 map charts major public transportation routes in the city's commercial center. One can readily see the Loop Elevated Railroad that still defines the downtown, as well as the several scattered passenger railroad stations that the planners hoped to replace with fewer, larger, and more efficient terminals. Other familiar landmarks that remain are the Marshall Field Store, the Chicago Public Library (now the Chicago Cultural Center), and the Art Institute. City Hall is in the same block as it is now, but the building outlined here was demolished and replaced with the current structure by 1911. Some street names have also changed. For example, Fifth Avenue is now Wells Street. American Society of Mechanical Engineers, Chicago Historical Society (ICHi-34342).

As the planners observed, the real estate market rather than efficiency determined the locations of railroad tracks, stations, and other facilities, though by the turn of the century the companies had accomplished some streamlining by shifting much freight handling outside the business center. Passenger trains moved workers and travelers in and out of downtown in staggering numbers. Carl Condit—the renowned historian of Chicago architecture, building, planning, and urban technology—counts 1,300 such trains a day in 1910 carrying a total of 175,000 passengers (ridership peaked at 270,000 a decade later) to and from the six principal downtown stations. With so many railroad tracks lacerating so much of the city at grade level, traffic delays and deadly accidents were part of the fabric of Chicago life.

The 1904 Special Park Commission pointed out that Chicago, once a leader in park construction, had fallen behind other cities in per capita acreage as well as in the convenience of location of the parks that did exist. The Lincoln Park Zoo (there was also an aquarium) and the conservatories in both Garfield Park and Lincoln Park were already established, however, by the early twentieth century. Lincoln Park had added three hundred acres to its original 150-acre expanse by dumping fill in the lake as far north as Belmont Avenue, and Grant Park approached its current size through the same method. The source of much of the fill was the Sanitary Canal dig. Through extensive re-landscaping, the South Park commissioners transformed Jackson Park, which had been the fairgrounds of the Columbian Exposition, into the kind of natural setting Frederick Law Olmsted had envisioned it becoming in his 1869 design.

Meanwhile, park and playground advocates were busy at work in new ventures both at Chicago's periphery and well within city limits. In 1903 the Cook County Board established the Outer Belt Commission, which evolved the following decade into the Forest Preserve District. By the time the *Plan of Chicago* appeared, Chicago had created several new parks and recreational facilities. These were smaller than the earlier major parks on the North, West, and South sides, and their locations were more accessible to many working people. According to the South Park Commission, in 1908 almost 5.8 million visitors enjoyed the indoor and outdoor gyms, pools, club and reading rooms, assembly halls, and lunch rooms in its thirteen small parks. The commission counted more than 2 million visits to its dozen playgrounds the same year. Among the new facilities was Sherman Park on the South Side, whose field house was designed by D. H. Burnham and Company. The park was named after Daniel Burnham's beloved father-in-law and former president of the commission, John B. Sherman, who had passed away in 1902.

According to the 1900 census, Chicago's population was 1,698,575. It passed 2 million by the time of the *Plan* and reached 2,185,183 in 1910. While the number of people living in the United States climbed by 21 percent between 1900 and 1910, the population of Cook County jumped 31 percent in the same decade. The Chicago the planners saw was larger than any other city in the world except London, New York, and Paris. The percentage of Chicagoans who had immigrated from abroad had peaked in the 1850s and 1860s at over half the city, but in 1910 it was still close to twice the rate of the country as a whole. Fully 35.7 percent of residents were foreign born, and another 41.8 percent, while native to America, had at least one parent from another country. Two percent of the city were African American. The absolute and relative numbers of African Americans would rapidly rise beginning with World War I. There were 1,788 Chinese in Chicago in 1910, 1,713 of them male. Of the foreign-born white population in 1910, almost a quarter were from Germany. The percentage of Germans was declining, as was that of immigrants from Ireland, while the representation from eastern Europe had rapidly risen. In 1909, 6,296 public schoolteachers taught 296,426 students. Chicago's mortality rate that year was 14.58 per thousand. More than 20 percent of the Chicagoans who died—6,384 out of 31,296—were children under a year old. Chicago was frequently healthier than other American cities, though rankings fluctuated from year to year. The leading causes of death were pneumonia, tuberculosis, heart disease, and, for infants, diarrhea.

Chicagoans worked in an extraordinarily wide range of circumstances, from lofty offices to basement sweatshops. Most found jobs in one of the city's nearly ten thousand manufacturing establishments. In 1909 six major industries—men's and women's clothing (by far the largest in number of workers), iron and steel forging and machine-shop products, printing and publishing, slaughtering and meatpacking, railroad-car manufacturing and repair, and electrical machinery—

employed more than 142,000 of Chicago's 294,000 wage earners. Heavy industry was concentrated along the North and South branches of the Chicago River and on the city's Southeast Side. The dreadful working conditions in the garment industry and, more sensationally, the packinghouses attracted attention nationwide, especially after the publication of Upton Sinclair's *The Jungle* in 1906.

Chicago was very much a union town and a place where class lines were sharply drawn, as they had been since at least the 1870s. Among many labor disputes in the years just before the publication of the *Plan of Chicago* were the especially bitter and violent stockyards strikes of 1902 and 1904, and the teamsters strike of 1905. The last dragged on over a hundred days and took the lives of fourteen people, including

FIGURE 16. The workers, and perhaps the owners, of Gerard & Rabe Clothing Manufacturers pose for their photograph outside the storefront factory, ca. 1880. Most of the workers are young and female. The man alone on the extreme right beyond a sign for a Chinese laundry appears to be himself Chinese. The Gerard & Rabe factory was located at what was, by Chicago's old numbering system, at 377 West Chicago Avenue, which now corresponds to 1413 West Chicago, just west of Noble Street on the Northwest Side. Chicago Historical Society (ICHi-38278).

FIGURE 17. This photograph of messenger boys during a strike in 1902 reveals how children were an important part of the workforce. Like bicycle messengers today, these boys were a speedy means of delivery between downtown offices. *Chicago Daily News,* Chicago Historical Society (DN-0000022).

two policemen. In June 1905 a few hundred anarchists, socialists, and left-wing trade unionists met in Chicago to form the Industrial Workers of the World. Big Bill Haywood called the convention to order by banging a wooden board on the podium, and Eugene Debs and Mother Jones were among those who addressed the delegates.

As reprehensible as were the circumstances in which many people worked, even worse were the places where poor Chicagoans lived, ate, and slept. While there were wards on the outer edges of Chicago inhabited by under ten people per acre, population density averaged over one hundred per acre in the slums of the Near West and Near Northwest sides. The overcrowding in some blocks exceeded four hundred persons per acre. The Investigating Committee of the City Homes Association, chaired by University of Chicago sociologist Robert Hunter and including Jane Addams, issued a scathing report in 1901 on slum housing. In *The Tenement Conditions in Chicago,* the committee claimed that the housing situation in the city was awful

FIGURE 18. This photograph (ca. 1900) of garbage in an alley in the Back of the Yards neighborhood near the packinghouses gives a sense of the kind of filth amidst which many working people in Chicago were forced to live. Chicago Historical Society (ICHi-34324).

and getting worse. They blamed not only greedy landlords but also "the short-sighted policy of the municipality which permits the growth of housing conditions for whose improvement years of agitation and vigorous effort will be necessary." The committee claimed that 300,000 Chicagoans were living in rear tenements jammed into the back of lots meant for one building and in inhumanly overpacked multi-level structures. These people were assaulted by the stench of privies, animal manure, and garbage, while deprived of decent light, air, and plumbing.

In 1911 Addams's Hull-House colleagues Sophonisba Breckinridge and Edith Abbott conducted a follow-up study in which they found that while the average population density in the city was 19.7 people per acre, in the worst wards it was five times that figure, and in several blocks 350 per acre or higher. While there were now a few sanitary reforms in force and the city had paved more streets and sidewalks since 1901, the overall "progress" was discouraging. "If there is little to be said of improvements during the last ten years,

there is much to be said of lack of improvements," Breckinridge and
Abbott concluded.

Chicago's cultural and political life was, like so many other things in
this city, rife with contrasts. By the time the *Plan* appeared, a new
public library (now the Chicago Cultural Center) and the current
homes of the Art Institute, the Chicago Symphony (Orchestra Hall
was designed by D. H. Burnham and Company), and the Newberry
Library had all been recently built. If 1909 Chicago could boast 21 libraries, 38 theaters, 750 newspapers and magazines, and 1,146 churches,
chapels, and missions, it also featured an infamous vice district in the
Near South Side's First Ward, as well as more than 7,000 saloons. In

FIGURE 19. The Chicago Historical Society was founded in 1856, but its first building and
virtually all of its early collections were lost in the Great Chicago Fire fifteen years later.
This structure, the society's third home, was built on the same site as the first two, at the
northwest corner of Dearborn and Ontario streets. After the Chicago Historical Society
moved to its present location at Clark Street and North Avenue in 1932, this building went
through a series of owners and uses, though the original name remains inscribed in stone
over the entrance. Barnes-Crosby, Chicago Historical Society (ICHi-19139).

FIGURE 20.   The Newberry Library, which was completed in 1892, is a private research library open to the public. Like the Chicago Historical Society building on Dearborn Street, it was designed by Henry Ives Cobb. It faces Walton Street and Washington Square Park, occupying the entire block between Dearborn and Clark streets. It was constructed on the site of the mansion of Mahlon D. Ogden, one of the very few buildings in the path of the Great Fire that survived. Barnes-Crosby, ca. 1905, Chicago Historical Society (ICHi-19099).

the same year, Chicago's 4,706 policemen made over 70,000 arrests that resulted in charges being brought. The leading felony was larceny, with 4,369 cases, but this figure did not even approach the number of arrests (43,398) for disorderly conduct. There were 73 murders, more than a hundred fewer than in 1905, though twenty more than in 1908.

Turn-of-the-century Chicago faced three significant political problems. The first two were logistical. The state constitution permitted cities only limited home rule powers, which made it difficult for municipalities to borrow money or undertake any other kind of action on major projects without explicit authorization from the state legislature. At the same time, several different separate local governments and boards exercised different but overlapping authority within

Chicago. For example, while Chicago residents constituted the over-whelming majority of residents of Cook County, the latter had (and still has) an independent government.

A much more colorful problem was a profoundly crooked group of representatives on the city council. Thanks to the efforts of reform groups such as the Civic Federation and the Municipal Voters League, and the deft if hardly flawless leadership of Carter Harrison II, mayor 1897–1905 and 1911–1915, better government advocates had accomplished considerable housecleaning. Muckraker Lincoln Steffens titled his chapter on local betterment efforts in *The Shame of the Cities* (1903) "Chicago: Half Free and Fighting On," which indicates correctly that victories were partial. For example, at the end of March 1909, the so-called Gray Wolves, a group of ethically challenged and politically powerful members of the Chicago City Council—including

FIGURE 21. The Art Institute of Chicago, seen here well before the first of several additions, opened on the east side of Michigan Avenue at Adams Street in 1892. It was designed by Shepley, Rutan, and Coolidge. This building was the site of several large intellectual and cultural conclaves that gathered in conjunction with the World's Columbian Exposition of 1893, and in July 1909 it hosted a special display of the *Plan of Chicago*. The firm of Burnham and Root was responsible for the previous home of the Art Institute, built in 1885 at 404 South Michigan Avenue. The Chicago Club took over that building when the Art Institute moved. Barnes-Crosby, Chicago Historical Society (ICHi-19219).

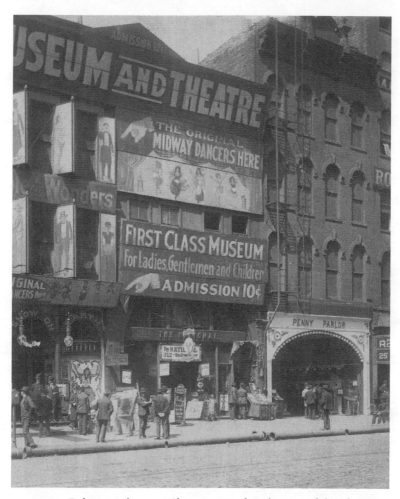

FIGURE 22. Early twentieth-century Chicago supported a wide variety of places for entertainment and recreation. Dime "museums" of curiosities, cheap theaters (one here claiming to feature "exotic" dancers from the Midway at Chicago's 1893 World's Columbian Exposition), and penny arcades catered to working people with limited means. The location is South State Street around 1912. Chicago Historical Society (ICHi-04793).

FIGURE 23. The fantastically castellated Coliseum at Fifteenth and Wabash was an all-purpose arena used for large-scale meetings, expositions, and sporting events. It survived well into the twentieth century. Numerous national political conventions took place there, including the one that nominated Republican William Howard Taft in 1908. Chicago Historical Society (ICHi-02018).

Johnny Powers, "Bathhouse" John Coughlin, Mike "Hinky Dink" Kenna, and Mike McInerney—lost 40–19 in a showdown vote on procedural changes backed by the Municipal Voters League. In its recommendations for the election a week later, the league declared Powers, Coughlin, Kenna, and McInerney as "totally unfit" for office, but they were reelected with only token opposition. Some advances were only temporary, as revealed by the election in 1915 of the corrupt buffoon William Hale "Big Bill" Thompson for the first of his three terms as mayor.

While they worked with elected leaders, the authors of the *Plan of Chicago* did not put much faith in such people. Daniel Burnham told the members of the Commercial Club in 1904 that the most pragmatic approach for them to take, if they wished to improve Chicago, was to raise on their own the considerable resources required to establish an independent organization that would force the city to act in a way it would not without external pressure, even if it had taxing and borrowing power. "The public authorities do not do their duty and they must be made to" was his steely advice. Whether this remark was based on practical experience, class prejudice, a different conception of the duty of public authorities than they themselves had—or all three—is difficult to ascertain precisely.

In any case, Burnham's observation reveals that in his more candid moments his view of the city's prospects was guarded. In several of his speeches and letters, and in the *Plan,* he expressed concern that Chicago's growth had reached the point of diminishing returns since increasing congestion and pollution were serious threats to continued commercial profits, the engine of urban vitality. Such comments displayed less than unqualified confidence in the future, as did his frequently reiterated contention that unless the city did something to make itself more attractive and efficient, businessmen and investors would move their money elsewhere. Working and living conditions also required attention. Chicago would not and could not expect to attract and keep the labor force required to power its industries and staff its offices unless it provided an appealing environment for everyone. Burnham recognized, perhaps more than he has been given credit for doing, that Chicago and America were places different from what they had been up to the 1890s, and that the future did not necessarily promise the same expansive patterns on which Bion Arnold had based his most bullish predictions.

Chicago's boosters and apologists eagerly maintained that the city still had plenty of room to grow. If it had shortcomings like dirt, disorder, and corruption, and if it was not as culturally sophisticated as the more established eastern cities, that was because Chicago was still like a strapping adolescent who had yet to reach maturity. The most well-known summoning of this metaphor is in Carl Sandburg's famous poem "Chicago," published just a few years after the *Plan of Chicago.* Sandburg likens the city to a tall and bold young "slugger," whose unrefined brashness and rough edges are part of his appeal. In many respects, the planners were far more forward-looking than

Sandburg. His view of the city, now an outdated cliché with no applicability to twenty-first-century Chicago, was arguably misleading even when he wrote it.

By the 1890s, and certainly by the time the planners set down to work, the city had reached very close to its full geographical limits, and its basic physical and economic structure was defined. Could it be that time was no longer the ally of Chicago, which had always counted on a bigger and better future? Investors within and outside the city were indeed looking for fresher centers of economic expansion farther to the west. Other cities were providing Chicago with stiff competition in its historically key industries, including lumber, grain, and even meatpacking. The automobile revolution was at hand, and the aviation age was on the horizon; both of these developments would pose challenges to the world's leading railroad city. Chicago continued to grow until the middle of the twentieth century, but not as quickly as its suburbs and some younger cities. The percentage of Chicagoans born outside the state and the country, while still substantial, continued to fall, and soon the outbreak of World War I and immigration restriction would considerably slow this influx of newcomers from abroad.

The planners could not foresee the war and its local consequences, of course, but they were convinced that it was no longer acceptable to dismiss the city's shortcomings as part of a phase from which it would soon naturally emerge all by itself. History was on Chicago's side only if people like themselves took effective action. It was time to do so.

CHAPTER FOUR

THE PLAN COMES TOGETHER

By the first decade of the twentieth century, two essential elements for redesigning Chicago were in place. There was a consensus among many influential and articulate people that important alterations in the city's built environment needed to be made, and there was some agreement, at least in a broad sense, regarding what those alterations should be. Numerous individuals and groups offered their recommendations in speeches, meetings, and publications. The *Plan of Chicago* stood out among all of these at the time, and it is the one set of proposals that has had the most far-ranging effects and is easily the best remembered. This is due not to the originality of its ideas, but to their comprehensiveness, the cogency with which they were expressed, and the exceptionally powerful position of those who supported them.

In every respect, the *Plan*'s defining qualities bear the imprint of the two main forces behind it, Daniel Burnham and the Commercial Club of Chicago. For Burnham, the *Plan* was the last and in many respects the greatest achievement in his extraordinary professional career. It reflects his remarkable combination of breadth of vision and grasp of salient detail, his ability to maintain a single-minded sense of purpose while juggling multiple daunting tasks, his commanding management style, and his intuitive sense of how to appeal to his clients' best sense of themselves. For the Commercial Club, remaking Chicago was the kind of project that resonated profoundly in its members' imaginations and made the fullest use of the knowledge and skills that had won them high positions among the city's business leaders and election to this exclusive organization.

Daniel Hudson Burnham was born on September 4, 1846, in Henderson, New York, on the eastern shore of Lake Ontario, southwest of Watertown. Burnham, who could trace his ancestry back to seventeenth-century Puritan New England, was the third son and fifth child of Edwin and Elizabeth Burnham, who moved their family to Chicago in 1855, where Edwin became a successful drug wholesaler. By the 1850s the place had become a metropolitan marvel whose vaunted prospects attracted many capable individuals. Daniel Burnham was of the second generation of Chicago's economic, political, and cultural elite. The first generation consisted of the so-called Old Settlers, who had arrived in the promising village mainly in the 1830s and 1840s. The second generation also included retailer Marshall Field

FIGURE 24. This impressive image of Burnham from around 1910 is the frontispiece of the worshipful two-volume biography published in 1921 by Charles Moore, with whom Burnham worked on the plan for Washington, D.C., and who edited the *Plan of Chicago*. Northwestern University Library.

and railroad-car manufacturer George Pullman, among others. Many, including Field and Pullman as well as Burnham, were from small-town New England or upstate New York.

Young Daniel Burnham was very uncertain about his future, but he appears to have discovered his calling in the fall of 1867 as a drafts-man in the firm of architect William Le Baron Jenney, one of the pioneers of the Chicago school of modern commercial architecture. Thrilled by Jenney's praise, Burnham wrote with pride and excite-ment to his mother, "I am perfectly in love with my profession," adding, "And for the first time in my life I feel perfectly certain that I have found my vocation." The following spring Burnham told her that he was resolved "to become the greatest architect in the city or country." In his correspondence with his mother, he also reaffirmed his belief—rooted in his upbringing in the Swedenborgian New Jerusalem Church—in the individual's free-willed ability to work for good. A typical business career, Burnham confided, was full of moral pitfalls. "But there can be none in a man's striving after the beautiful and useful laws God has created to govern his material uni-verse," he wrote, "and when I am trying to find them and apply them to use among my fellows He will reveal them and expand my mind and heart toward himself and all mankind." This outlook shaped Burnham's entire professional and public life.

As sure as he seemed to have been about the merits of his job, Burnham nevertheless left the drafting table in 1869 to try his luck at mining in Nevada, which had been admitted to the Union only five years before, and in his brief residence in the West he even made a failed run for the state senate. This diversion from his recent decision to become an architect may reflect less an inconstancy of purpose than it does a common pattern of the times, when many young men dabbled in often very different careers in scattered places before settling down. Both Pullman and Chicago meatpacker Philip D. Armour, for example, had similar experiences in the West. Once back in Chicago, Burnham resumed his architectural work. In the firm of Carter, Drake and Wight, he met another young, talented, and ambitious employee, John Wellborn Root. By 1873, the year Burnham turned twenty-seven and Root twenty-three, the two men had formed their own partnership.

Burnham and Root's major break came when John B. Sherman hired them to design his home on Prairie Avenue at Twenty-first Street. This turned out to be an especially important job, since Burnham married Sherman's daughter Margaret in 1876. As noted, Sherman was a major figure in the establishment of Chicago as a livestock sales and slaughtering center. He also had a long tenure on the South Park Commission and became a close personal adviser to his son-in-law. The Burnhams lived with the Shermans until Daniel and Margaret moved to their own home at Michigan Avenue and Forty-third Street. Through the remainder of the 1870s, Burnham and Root designed houses for numerous prominent Chicagoans. Their work also included the Union Stock Yard's landmark bull's-head gate at Exchange Avenue and Peoria Street, the only remnant today of this once-vast enterprise in which Sherman had played a principal role. By the 1880s the young architects' projects included schools, stores, and factories. At this time they started designing the public and commercial buildings that earned them their enduring place among the founders of the modern architecture for which Chicago became celebrated.

This work began with the ten-story Montauk Block (1882) at Monroe and Dearborn streets, often called the first skyscraper, and several structures that still grace Chicago. These include the Rookery Building (1888) at LaSalle and Adams, where Burnham and Root located their firm, and the Monadnock Building (1891) at Jackson and Dearborn. They did work in other cities, but Chicagoans remained their main clients. Burnham and Root's commissions included park buildings, railroad terminals, banks, and hotels, not to mention the original home of the Art Institute of Chicago (1887) at Michigan and Van Buren. Their Rand-McNally Building (1890), on Adams Street between LaSalle and Quincy, was the first all steel-frame skyscraper.

While Root was the primary designer in the partnership, Burnham determined many of the important general guidelines in the plans the firm produced. He also furnished the organizational, administrative, and promotional skills crucial to finding and satisfying

FIGURE 25. The Rookery, built in 1885–86 and still standing on the southeast corner of LaSalle and Adams streets, is a magnificently detailed combination of iron framing and masonry bearing walls. Barnes-Crosby, ca. 1905, Chicago Historical Society (ICHi-19186).

clients, coordinating responsibilities within the office, and executing buildings of quality and distinction. In 1886 Burnham, now a prosperous man, moved his family—he and Margaret had two daughters and three sons—to a sixteen-room house on a six-acre wooded plot by the lakefront in Evanston. This champion of city life explained in another letter to his mother, "I did it because I can no longer bear to have my children run in the streets of Chicago, and because especially I can not stand them being on the South Side." The spacious house and grounds, which the Burnhams altered a good deal over the years, were the center of their full and contented domestic life. Burnham and Root's highly successful and harmonious partnership came to a premature end with Root's death at forty-one in 1891, during preliminary planning for the World's Columbian Exposition. Burnham reorganized the firm into D. H. Burnham and Company, which received more than two hundred commissions, most of them for large structures, by the time of Burnham's own passing in 1912.

Among D. H. Burnham and Company's major works that are still extant are the Reliance Building (1895, first plan by Root—converted in 1999 to the Hotel Burnham) at the southwest corner of Washington

FIGURE 26. In 1888 Burnham and Root moved their firm from their Montauk Building to the Rookery, where, not long before Root's death in 1891, they sat for this carefully posed portrait that shows their partnership and practice as solid, successful, and civilized. Chicago Historical Society (ICHi-37303).

and State streets, portions of the Marshall Field and Company Store (1892, with several subsequent additions) diagonally across the street, and Orchestra Hall (1905) on Michigan Avenue south of Adams Street. The firm designed the Railway Exchange Building (1904, now the Santa Fe Building), just south of Orchestra Hall, and moved its office there. Notable D. H. Burnham and Company buildings outside of Chicago include the Flatiron Building (1902) in New York, Union Station (1907) in Washington, D.C., and the John Wanamaker department store in Philadelphia—the sumptuous retail palace whose 1909 grand opening was attended by President William Howard Taft.

FIGURE 27. Burnham constructed this cabin on the Wooded Island of the World's Columbian Exposition (some fair buildings are visible behind the cabin) so that he could literally live with the all-consuming project. This photograph appears in Charles Moore's biography of Burnham, along with a caption that mentions the "artists' revels," a reference to the sometimes high-spirited doings among Burnham and his fellow architects and artists before they went to bed on the cots in the cabin. "Merrily sped the hours with jests and stories and practical jokes by the painters and sculptors," Moore writes, "and on Sunday evenings there was music by a band made up from Theodore Thomas's Orchestra, with the master himself to direct them." Northwestern University Library.

FIGURE 28. This picture of Burnham and some of his key associates on the project was likely taken the winter before the fair opened. The enormous structures of the Court of Honor loom in the background. From left to right: Ernest R. Graham, assistant director of works; unidentified; Burnham; M. B. Pickett, secretary of works; unidentified; and Charles B. Atwood, who designed several fair buildings. Chicago Historical Society (ICHi-02208).

Burnham's engagement in the kind of projects that led to the *Plan of Chicago* began with his supervision of the design and construction of the World's Columbian Exposition. However one assesses the fair, it is impossible not to be impressed by Burnham's almost superhuman drive and managerial ability on this colossal effort. He moved into a cabin on the site in Jackson Park, from which he directed the activities of dozens of artisans and hundreds of workers. His dedication and determination were so prodigious that it seems almost as if he lifted the immense buildings from the mud and slush by an act of personal will. As the May 1 opening date of the fair approached, he wrote to Margaret, "The intensity of this last month is very great indeed. You can little imagine it. I am surprised at my own calmness under it all." He regretted that very few of the men constructing the fair met his high standards. "The rest have to be pounded every hour of the day, and they are the ones who make me tired," he confessed with impatience and fatigue.

Burnham was and remained immensely proud of the results—he installed the fireplace from the Jackson Park cabin in his house in Evanston—and of the praise he received for his achievement. Even before the fair opened, architects and other cultural leaders in New York saluted his achievement at a dinner in that city. The Association of American Architects elected him its president in 1893 and 1894. In the latter year, Northwestern University awarded him an honorary doctorate, while Harvard and Yale, which young Daniel Burnham had unsuccessfully aspired to attend, acknowledged his accomplishments with honorary master's degrees.

While working on the fair, Burnham developed some of the most important personal and professional relationships of his career, notably with architects Charles F. McKim (of the New York firm of McKim, Mead and White) and Charles B. Atwood, and with sculptor Augustus Saint-Gaudens. Burnham brought Atwood into his practice to assume many of the design duties that Root formerly performed. Burnham the fair builder established certain work methods that he followed in future planning endeavors. He set up shop for the plan of San Francisco, as he had done in Jackson Park, in a temporary structure atop Twin Peaks, from which he and his staff could view the object of their labors. For the *Plan of Chicago,* he ordered a special penthouse constructed on the roof of the Railway Exchange Building that provided a panorama of the city below.

Burnham learned a great deal from the succession of planning projects after the fair. During their time together in Washington, D.C., McKim demonstrated to Burnham how the preparation and display of well-drawn architectural illustrations could help win public support. Burnham also continued to make key contacts. He met Charles Moore, secretary to Michigan senator James McMillan, who was chair of the Senate District of Columbia Committee. Moore later served as editor of the *Plan of Chicago* and wrote the first biography of Burnham. In his entire planning career, the only time Burnham accepted a fee was for the Cleveland plan, and he evidently did so in order not to embarrass his associates John M. Carrère and Arnold W. Brunner, who, unlike Burnham, needed the income. One aspect of Burnham's administrative acumen was his ability to entrust the day-

FIGURE 29. The Railway Exchange Building (now the Santa Fe Building) opened in 1904 at 224 South Michigan Avenue. Among previous occupants of the site were the stables for the Palmer House hotel. The Railway Exchange is the central building in this 2004 view of Michigan Avenue from across the Illinois Central tracks in Grant Park. It is flanked by the former Straus Building to the south and the Borg-Warner Building to the north. Orchestra Hall, designed by D. H. Burnham and Company, is between the Borg-Warner and Railway Exchange buildings, obscured by the trees. Barely visible, to the right of the Santa Fe sign, is the "penthouse" Burnham had built as the space where the *Plan of Chicago* was to be prepared. This was also where many visitors were brought to view the work-in-progress. Harlan Wallach, Academic Technologies, Northwestern University.

to-day management of D. H. Burnham and Company to others while still watching that the jobs kept coming and that the office completed them successfully.

Burnham complained occasionally about the amount of time he spent away from his own practice. He often tried to make sure that expenses were covered, however, and that others who worked with him were suitably compensated. For instance, Edward Bennett received a salary of $600 a month while assigned to the *Plan of Chicago*. It is also likely that the prestige and visibility of the planning projects benefited D. H. Burnham and Company. But it would be a disservice to Burnham to undervalue in any way the countless hours and all the thought, labor, and personal substance he donated to these projects, as well as the sincerity and idealism with which he approached them.

Viewed in retrospect, the alliance of Daniel Burnham with the men of the Merchants Club and Commercial Club to create the *Plan of Chicago* appears natural to the point of inevitable. Burnham was, after all, very much one of them, having been elected to the Commercial Club in 1901, and he shared the Republican politics of the members of both organizations, their pride in their personal achievements, their belief in the efficacy of decisive action, and their commitment to Chicago, as demonstrated by their extensive service on the boards of multiple civic, cultural, and charitable organizations. He also shared their high-intentioned if sometimes self-righteous trust in their own motives and ideas. Like them, he saw no conflict between his (and their) best interests and those of the city as a whole.

The Commercial Club dates to 1877, when thirty-nine leading businessmen, inspired by a visit to Chicago by members of the Commercial Club of Boston, founded their own similar organization. They defined their central purpose as "advancing by social intercourse and by a friendly interchange of views the prosperity and growth of the city of Chicago." The club limited its membership—the original number was sixty—to men representing a range of commercial interests. They convened regularly at the Chicago Club and similar venues (the Commercial Club never constructed a building of its own) for business meetings, followed by dinner and discussions that usually featured presentations by an invited speaker or speakers, often one or more of their own members. The schedule varied over the years, but the form and purpose of the meetings remained fundamentally the same.

Qualifications for nomination and election included what the official history of the club calls "conspicuous success." In choosing new members, the club also looked for "interest in the general welfare" evidenced "by a record of things actually done and of liberality, as well as by willingness to do more," not to mention "a broad and comprehending sympathy with important affairs of city and state, and a generous subordinating of self in the interests of the community." Membership carried with it rigorous requirements for attendance at meetings and participation in the club's initiatives. The Merchants Club, founded in 1896, had much the same size, purpose, and structure as the Commercial Club, though its roster was intentionally younger since only men under forty-five were eligible for election. A major motivation for the clubs' merger in 1907 was to join forces to create a plan for Chicago.

The speaker lists of the clubs—dominated by statesmen, politicians, academics, scientists, clergymen, experts, reformers, and cultural leaders of high achievement and reputation—reflect their memberships' power and prestige, and also their abiding interest in the well-being of the city they had helped make and that had rewarded them so amply. Among the topics of the Commercial Club's first year of meetings were "Compromise with Fraud," "The Situation of Our Municipal Affairs," and "Our City Streets," as well as current trade and taxation policies. The members took up other thorny matters, such as pollution, unemployment, labor violence, and, at a meeting of the Merchants Club at which the noted African American educator and spokesman Booker T. Washington spoke, "The Negro Problem in the South." Both clubs were addressed by presidents of the United States. The Merchants Club also invited New York–based reformer Jacob Riis to share with them his thoughts on the playground movement, while the Commercial Club hosted Jane Addams on the same topic.

By the time of the *Plan of Chicago,* the collective memberships identified among their most important work the founding of the Chicago Manual Training School and other similar institutions aimed at assisting Chicago's working class, reducing the costs of loans taken out by wage earners, public school reform, establishment of the Chicago Sanitary District, exposure and punishment of crooked local officials, helping stage the World's Columbian Exposition, and donating to the federal, state, and city government, respectively, the sites for Fort Sheridan and the Great Lakes Naval Training Station, the Second Regiment Armory, and a new playground on the Northwest Side.

As the *Plan* neared completion, the Commercial Club published a promotional document that listed thirty-two of its members, including Daniel Burnham, as having contributed significantly to its creation. The similarities among these men, and the differences between them and most Chicagoans, are noteworthy. As a general rule, they worked in close proximity to each other in the central downtown and lived in tight clusters either along the Gold Coast on the North Side or Prairie Avenue on the South Side. A few, like Burnham, made their homes in the suburbs, mainly in towns north of the city. Most were top executives in heavy industry, large-scale wholesaling, or banking and finance. Their average age in 1909, the year the *Plan* appeared, was fifty-two, though two of the central figures in its creation, Charles D. Norton and Clyde M. Carr, were thirty-eight and forty (Burnham turned sixty-three in 1909).

They did resemble a large number of their fellow citizens in that many of them were not originally from Chicago. Only nine of the thirty-two were born in the city, and fourteen did not arrive until they were at least twenty years old. There the resemblance between their backgrounds and those of most of the populace ended. Thirty-one were born in the United States, and the one exception (Frederic A. Delano) was born in Hong Kong to American parents. Virtually all were Protestant and Republican, and every one was white and male. Twenty of them (not including Burnham) had attended college at a time when higher education was not nearly as common an experience as it is now. Ten went to Harvard, Yale, or Princeton. Twenty-seven were listed in the 1906 Chicago *Social Register*.

They shared membership not only in the Commercial Club but also on corporate boards and in numerous other business, social, cultural, and golf clubs. Seventeen belonged to the Union League Club, nineteen to the University Club. Burnham was a member of both of these organizations as well as three literary and arts clubs (the Caxton Club, the Little Room, and the Cliff Dwellers) and two golf clubs (Evanston and Glenview). They also had joined various professional organizations, such as the American Bar Association, and an impressive list of charitable, social service, and cultural boards. Eight were on the board of the Chicago Symphony, for example, and twelve on that of the Art Institute of Chicago. Such public-spirited activity was not only a requirement for membership in the Commercial Club, but also one of many overlapping and mutually reinforcing connections among those in this extraordinarily influential, tightly knit, and like-minded group.

The members of both the Commercial and Merchants clubs believed in the ethos of the City Beautiful movement. They were certainly aware of the proposal that Burnham had put before the South Park commissioners, at the prompting of commission president James Ellsworth, to use landfill to construct a downtown lakefront recreational area connected by a lagoon and a parkway to Jackson Park. Ellsworth was a charter member of the Merchants Club. In February 1897 Burnham spoke to this group on "The Needs of a Great City" at the first meeting after it was organized. He was back less than two months later to talk about "The Improvements of the South Shore." A week before that, he and Ellsworth had discussed the question of "What Can Be Done to Make Chicago More Attractive?" at a meeting of the Commercial Club.

In 1901 wholesale grocer Franklin MacVeagh, a former president of the Commercial Club and a mainstay of several other civic-minded organizations, first proposed that Burnham and the club combine to consider how the city's built environment could be improved. Little came of this proposal in Burnham's own city, though he meanwhile developed his ideas for Washington, Cleveland, San Francisco, and Manila. Burnham spoke again before the Merchants Club in February 1903, however, on "The Lake Front." That summer Merchants Club members Delano and Norton asked club president Walter H. Wilson to organize a dinner to honor Burnham and his fellow Washington planners. Delano was general manager (soon president) of the Wabash Railroad, and he later served as chairman of the National Resources Planning Commission in his nephew Franklin Delano Roosevelt's administration. Life insurance executive Norton would become chief assistant to MacVeagh after the latter was appointed secretary of the treasury under Taft. Wilson worked in banking and real estate. An undisguised purpose of the dinner was to drum up interest in developing a plan for Chicago. Wilson agreed to manage this event, but Burnham caused its cancellation since discussions of implementing the Washington plan were at a politically delicate stage.

The Merchants Club persisted. In the summer of 1906, another of their members, *Chicago Tribune* publisher Joseph Medill McCormick, talked with Burnham about creating a plan for Chicago. This conversation took place as both were aboard a train carrying them home from San Francisco, where Burnham had been trying without success to convince authorities in the post-earthquake city to adopt his plan for it. Burnham was intrigued, but he advised McCormick that "the work contemplated will be an enormous job." In Burnham's opinion, Chicago's acceptance of a plan could "only be brought about after a hard fight by some public spirited organization." No organizations were better suited than the Merchants and Commercial clubs, however, since they represented the "property interests" that would be most affected.

Alerted by McCormick, Delano and Norton approached Burnham right away. Burnham told them that courtesy required him to speak with MacVeagh. He did so, and MacVeagh responded that he was "extremely glad" to hear that members of the Merchants Club had pursued the idea of a plan "for Chicago's development and security, in the present and future, along lines of beauty and convenience." He was also delighted that Burnham was willing to work with them. "You are the man," MacVeagh assured Burnham, "and that, as you well know, I have all the while perfectly understood." The Commercial Club was at the moment preoccupied with finding a site for the Field Museum, a matter complicated by Marshall Field's death in January 1906. MacVeagh said that he "heartily approved" of letting the Merchants Club take the lead. Speaking for his colleagues at the Commercial Club, he assured Burnham that "what we all wish is to get you at work—and to accomplish the thing." Burnham shared MacVeagh's letter with Norton, informing him, "I am now ready whenever you are."

Burnham, who by this time was arguably the most experienced urban planner in the country, considered what he would require. He prepared a memo saying he needed plenty of office space, a chief assistant (the position Bennett would assume), and as much help, "expert and routine," as the job demanded. As for how to proceed, Burnham stated, "General studies to scale should be made until by logical exclusion, a general plan plainly justifying itself shall have been worked out." The details would follow. Even at this preliminary stage, when work on the actual design had not even begun, Burnham looked ahead to "the presentation of it in large and in small, by plans, sections, bird's-eye views." He recommended that "finally, the whole thing should be printed with complete illustrations." Burnham also specified that he would be indisputably in charge and would report to the club alone, though he would consult with others as the need arose.

Meanwhile, Norton discussed with the Executive Committee of the Merchants Club how to estimate costs, as well as how to galvanize the membership and the city into action. He suggested that a group of members, himself included, might get things under way by agreeing to underwrite the project, their financial commitment to be reduced by the amount that other individuals subsequently subscribed. On September 17, the Executive Committee endorsed the proposal and entrusted Norton, Delano, and Wilson to take the lead. By October 1, the three had hammered out the substance of an agreement with Burnham, who advised them about which individuals to keep informed and to invite to a forthcoming banquet at which the project would be announced. The list included colleagues and acquaintances from Burnham's earlier planning work, numerous congressmen, and other federal officeholders. "The presence of the national officials," Burnham explained, "will help the Washington, as well as the Chicago[,] work, and the occasion is sure to bring about a realization of the seriousness of the peoples' purpose to do away with disorder and to substitute civic beauty and convenience."

The Executive Committee of the Merchants Club called for a closed meeting on October 19 at which the prospective plan for Chicago was one of two major agenda items (the other was reform of the administration of the public schools). The committee members hoped that the club would endorse the project "on the understanding that such approval commits every member to give his enthusiastic support and co-operation" to Finance Committee chair Wilson. This meant pledging funds and, very possibly, joining the planning effort. They estimated that $25,000 was the minimum sum required to produce a plan, and that substantially more would be needed to promote its implementation after it was released. While Wilson and others who were committed to the project agreed to guarantee financing, they continued to expect that individual contributions from members and the broader public would be generous.

The call to the October 19 Merchants Club meeting reminded members that as many as half the businessmen in Chicago had only recently arrived in the city. Such newcomers had heard too many pessimistic forecasts about Chicago's condition and "too few concrete constructive propositions laid before them to appeal to their imagination and hope and to increase their civic pride and loyalty." A "big imaginative Plan" would inspire them. The public was clearly interested in "an orderly and beautiful development of cities" and believed in the practical value of such development. In Daniel Burnham, Chicago possessed "a great civic asset." The moment was right. At the meeting Norton read a letter from utilities magnate Samuel Insull promising $1,000, and another from dry-goods wholesaler Edward Butler pledging the same amount, with a guarantee of $4,000 more. The Executive Committee's proposal carried the day. The *Plan* had a plan.

CHAPTER FIVE

CREATING THE PLAN

The *Plan of Chicago* is commonly referred to as the Burnham Plan, which is certainly appropriate, though only up to a point. Daniel Burnham's stature as a city planner and his active interest in remaking Chicago were indispensable to inspiring this project and then bringing it to successful completion. Once he was hired by the Merchants Club, which soon after merged with the Commercial Club under the latter's name, Burnham directed the work and, more than anyone else, shaped the *Plan of Chicago*'s contents and form. But creating the *Plan* was an immensely complex undertaking that included the efforts of many people. One of its milestone achievements was the formation of a new kind of alliance (though there was a precedent in the San Francisco plan) between businessmen and a commercial architect with the purpose of making comprehensive changes in the structure of a major city. A similar collaboration in Chicago had produced the Columbian Exposition, but that had also included government involvement. And, as impressive as was the exposition, the scope of the *Plan of Chicago*'s ambitions was of a far greater magnitude.

The members of the Merchants and Commercial clubs were very successful men of affairs who were accustomed to dealing with large-scale enterprises. They also had, individually and collectively, an extraordinary record of constructive civic engagement. They commissioned Burnham to lead them because, as Franklin MacVeagh had observed, he had demonstrated that he was so obviously the right man for this particular project. His firm had designed the buildings in which many of their set lived and worked, he had overseen the construction of the fair that had done Chicago so proud, and he had prepared plans for other major metropolises. Indeed, Burnham's multiple accomplishments had put the idea of remaking Chicago in their minds in the first place. They trusted his judgment, shared his vision, and admired his reputation for achieving great things.

But they had staked a claim every bit as good as his that Chicago was their city. They were as prepared as was he to show their commitment to Chicago, they believed that they were as qualified to act in what they saw as its best interests, and both they and he knew that their participation and backing were crucial to the creation and implementation of any plan on this scale. It is unlikely, however, that when they began their work they knew just how demanding a task they had set for themselves and how large a commitment was required.

The planners met formally several hundred times over the thirty months prior to the publication of the *Plan* on July 4, 1909. They also held countless informal discussions in person and by telephone during and outside business hours, and they exchanged hundreds of notes, telegrams, and letters among themselves. They could honestly state at the close of the *Plan* that it was the product of "a systematic and comprehensive study . . . with the sole purpose of mapping out an ideal for the physical development of the city." While they did not claim "perfection of detail," they were sure enough of the value of what they had done to declare that they could place the *Plan of Chicago* before the public "in the confident belief that it points the way to realize civic conditions of unusual economy, convenience, and beauty."

Daniel Burnham was not present on October 29, 1906, as six members of the Merchants Club convened for the first meeting on preparing the plan authorized by the club. At that point they had yet to decide what to call the committee on which they were serving. The typed minutes of the meeting leave a space for its title. Someone has handwritten in this space "(Name to be decided)." Soon they would be the Committee on the Plan of Chicago. After the merger of the clubs early in 1907, there would be a larger General Committee, members of which would chair subcommittees on specific parts of the city that the *Plan* would address: the lakefront, the boulevard to connect the North and South sides, and railway terminals. By 1908 these had evolved into committees on lake parks, streets and boulevards, interurban roadways, and finance, as well as railway terminals. The planners devoted their first and several succeeding meetings to figuring out how to raise the money required to produce a plan. Burnham meanwhile took charge of two other areas: defining and prioritizing the key elements of Chicago that the planners would address and gathering the relevant information necessary to understand current conditions and calculate projections about the future. The committee members shared with him the demanding duties of lobbying local and state political and business leaders for the purpose of

FIGURE 30. Several of the key planners pose here during a meeting and a meal in 1908 in Burnham's Railway Exchange Building office. Starting from the left and going clockwise around the table, they are Edward B. Butler, Burnham, Charles D. Norton, Clyde M. Carr, Edward F. Carry, Edward H. Bennett, John DeLaMater, Charles G. Dawes, Charles H. Wacker, John V. Farwell, John W. Scott, Emerson B. Tuttle, Theodore W. Robinson, Charles H. Thorne, and John G. Shedd. Behind them are illustrations from the *Plan*. Chicago Historical Society (ICHi-03560).

encouraging their support (or at least reducing their opposition) to what the club would propose. They also assisted him in attempting to control when, how, and among whom the planners' work would be publicized. If Burnham was not at the first meeting, he was the dominant presence at many others. He hosted dozens of these sessions in the offices of D. H. Burnham and Company on the fourteenth floor of the Railway Exchange Building. He put a small team of draftsmen to work under the supervision of Bennett in the special rooms he had constructed on the roof of the building, overlooking Michigan Avenue, Grant Park, and, slightly to the north, the Art Institute.

In order to plan fund-raising, the Merchants Club pressed Burnham for an estimate of costs, which he submitted just before Christmas 1906. He told them he would contribute his own time gratis and would limit expenses to $25,000 for everything but the cost of editing and publishing a final report and then presenting it to the public. Burnham's production charges ended up being about $10,000 higher, mostly because the *Plan* was much broader in its scope than originally anticipated and took sixteen months longer than expected to complete. According to an accounting the General Committee made in December 1908, Burnham volunteered $10,000 out of his own pocket toward the cost of printing the *Plan* "in more attractive form and with ample illustrations in color," and for hiring Charles Moore, who had edited the Washington plan, to help write and edit the *Plan of Chicago*. The total production expenses by the time of publication were approximately $80,000.

The club's main strategy to pay for all these expenses was to sign up subscribers. To do this, it took full advantage of its well-heeled members and their networking ability. In exchange for contributions, fund-raisers offered subscribers the prestige of being associated with this effort and the satisfaction of having demonstrated their civic faith and loyalty. With remarkable speed, the subscription campaign reached its initial target of finding three hundred people who would pledge $100 each. By the end of 1907, the planners were asking for additional pledges of $300 spread over three years. Their target was now $100,000, which they calculated as the cost not only of finishing the *Plan* but also then publicizing it sufficiently to win endorsement by the city.

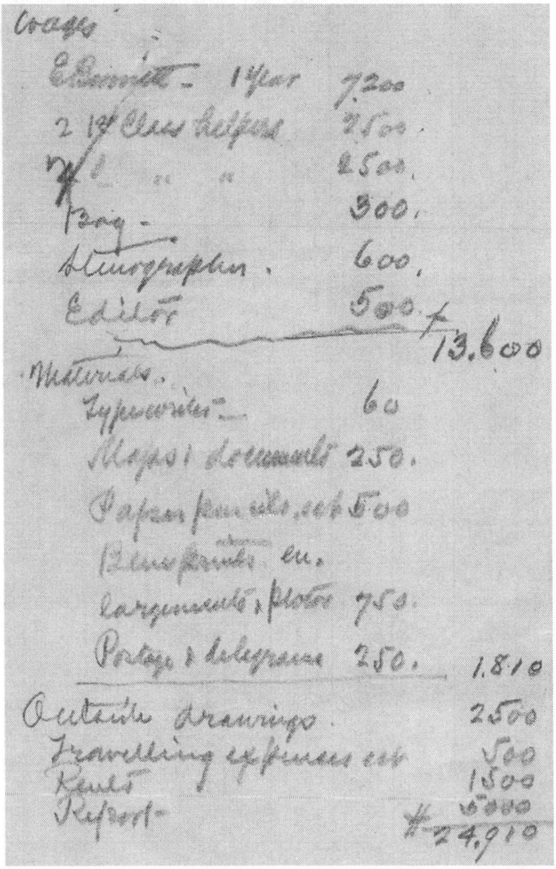
Wages
E. Bennett – 1 year 7200
2 1st Class helpers 2500
1 " " " 2500
Boy – 300
Stenographer 600
Editor 500
13.600
Materials
Typewriter 60
Maps & documents 250
Paper pencils, etc 500
Blue prints etc.
Enlargements & photos 750
Postage & telegrams 250
1.810
Outside drawings 2500
Travelling expenses etc 500
Rents 1500
Report 5000
$24,910

FIGURE 31. In Burnham's early handwritten notes on estimated costs, the biggest single item is Bennett's salary ($7,200 a year), which Burnham thought would be more than half the wages required. The creation of the drawings he was convinced were vital to getting public support for the proposals is also a significant item ($2,500), as is the preparation of the final report ($5,000). Note that Burnham also includes a charge for rent of the space on top of the Railway Exchange Building ($1,500). He removed some of the items listed here in the more formal estimate he submitted to the Merchants Club. The *Plan* ended up taking over two and a half years to prepare (rather than the one year assumed here), and it cost a little more than three times the total of this preliminary estimate. Daniel H. Burnham, letter to Charles Norton, November 21, 1906. Edward H. Bennett Collection, Ryerson and Burnham Archives, The Art Institute of Chicago. Reproduction © The Art Institute of Chicago.

There were a few petty squabbles among these practical men of means over precise costs for this and that, and over who should pay for what, even including some testy correspondence about the price of the lunches served at meetings in Burnham's office. The unity, dedication, and generosity of these strong-minded individuals were remarkable, however. When funds grew tight, the core leadership agreed among themselves to cover expenses, whether or not these were defrayed by additional contributions from subscribers. According to the financial report the planners drew up in December 1908, one unnamed member made a "special contribution" of $10,000 "in order that the Committee might be free to develop the Plan along the broadest lines."

Develop it along these lines they did. By early 1907 work was in full swing. Burnham sent out scores of letters locally and nationally to individuals, offices, and agencies asking for figures on the height of the masts of ships that navigated the Chicago River; the miles of railroad tracks within the city; the specifications of street grades; the volume of passengers and freight that moved in, out, and through Chicago; and any number of other things. He wrote to American consuls abroad for maps and technical information on the layout of major cities in Europe and Asia. He received many inquiries, as well as solicited and unsolicited advice, from across the country. On Burnham's behalf and on their own, others also gathered information. For example, Charles D. Norton, who served as chair of the General Committee through all of its permutations, asked University of Chicago political science professor Charles Merriam, an outspoken advocate of local government reform, to prepare an estimate of how much money the city of Chicago had spent on capital improvements in the twenty-five years between 1881 and 1906. Norton's purpose was to show how much more economically the city could fund improvements with a master plan than without one.

Burnham and the members of the several *Plan* committees liberally exercised their considerable political clout. They discussed among themselves what laws needed to be drafted or amended, whose support they required, and how best to persuade these people. To this end, they compiled lists of local and state elected officials and commission heads. They created advisory bodies consisting of Illinois governor Charles Deneen, Chicago mayor Fred Busse, numerous aldermen, and the officers of the Drainage Board, the Board of Education, the Art Institute, the Chicago Commercial Association, the park commissions, the Western Society of Engineers, and the American Institute of Architects, among other organizations. They invited many such worthies to contribute their wisdom and experience to the planning effort. The planners were shrewd enough to hear out and not simply ignore or dismiss those with opposing views. Realizing that certain politicians and businessmen might feel that their interests were being neglected, the committee chairs tried to reassure them. For instance, Clyde Carr, chair of the committee dealing with the proposed Michigan Boulevard, told Burnham that he asked the president of the Real Estate Board to stop by Burnham's office to receive a personal update, "as I am anxious to have all the support possible from this Real Estate Board."

On occasion the planners traveled to Springfield to confer with state officials. They had a special interest in the charter reform referendum of September 17, 1907, which, if successful, would increase local authority in ways Republican businessmen like the members of the Commercial Club favored. This measure was defeated by the voters, however. Early in 1907 the planners organized a discussion with the commissioners of the South Park board, whose approval they needed for any proposals affecting the lakefront from Grant Park south. In the fall of the same year, they started arranging special viewings of their work to date in the Railway Exchange rooftop drafting rooms for those they wished to impress. Among the organizations they hosted were the Industrial Club (with which the Commercial Club merged in 1932) and the Chicago Association of Commerce. On October 30 they waited upon the mayor, the corporation counsel, the chair of the board of local improvements, and First Ward aldermen Mike "Hinky Dink" Kenna and "Bathhouse" John Coughlin. The inclusion of politicians whose scruples many reformers and, doubtless, members of the Commercial Club found highly dubious indicates how flexible and pragmatic the planners were in their efforts to generate support for their work.

At the other end of the city's political spectrum from Kenna and Coughlin was Jane Addams, with whom they also consulted. Addams was among the many West Siders the planners polled on the widening of Halsted Street. According to an internal summary of her response, Addams said Hull-House would not oppose the change "if it were a part of a well considered scheme for the general improvement of the city." Small as her role was in shaping the *Plan of Chicago,* Addams was among the very few women who had any part at all in the preparation of the *Plan.* This is, regrettably, not surprising, since very few Chicago women ran large businesses and, until 1914, none could vote. What is remarkable, however, is the extent to which prominent people like Addams and even the mayor and governor seemed to concede the authority of Burnham and other members of the Commercial Club—who were a few dozen individuals in a small private organization—to propose major changes that affected all Chicagoans.

Burnham devoted himself to the project with his characteristic enthusiasm and energy. He sometimes changed appointments and travel arrangements to accommodate planning meetings. But he did not work full-time on the *Plan of Chicago.* He traveled to Europe in the spring of 1907 and again the following year, he continued to meet with his firm's clients, and he lost several weeks because of health problems. When Burnham was not immediately available, Bennett often acted as his intermediary, though Burnham remained unquestionably in charge. Bennett, who lived several towns north of Evanston in Lake Forest, sometimes stayed over at Burnham's home on Sunday evenings so they could talk about progress to date. They would continue their conversation on the way into Chicago the next morning.

Bennett's recollections reveal that while Burnham emphasized the need to consider all the possible solutions to different problems and the many details that each alternative involved, he kept his and his associates' focus always on the big picture. At a meeting of the main *Plan* committee in September 1908, when the work was nearing completion, Burnham passionately advised against compromising their key recommendations because of anticipated opposition or other complications. He told his colleagues that he "objected very much to having anything but the best thing," maintaining that "it is better

FIGURE 32. Edward H. Bennett. A portrait of the planner
as a young man. Northwestern University Library.

to wait for years and have the best than to take something unfit and
having to do the whole thing over again."

These colleagues responded with similar thoroughness and zeal.
Frederic Delano wrote to Carr that the latter's committee on the proposed Michigan Boulevard "should leave no stone unturned to push
the thing through." Several ideas expressed in the *Plan of Chicago*
originated with Commercial Club members other than Burnham.
Edward Butler, who chaired the Committee on the Lake Front (later
the Lake Parks), had for several years been considering how to improve this portion of the city. Railroad executive Delano had previously prepared a report on reorganizing rail service in Chicago. The
work pace of the committee members naturally ebbed and flowed
with the shifting demands of such an enormous and multipart undertaking. In an apparent moment of weariness perhaps induced by
the defeat of charter reform, Charles Norton suggested at the meeting a week after the failed referendum that perhaps now "there was
little for the Committee to do except to attend such meetings as

Mr. Burnham might request for the purpose." The high level of Norton's and others' subsequent involvement in the planning indicates, however, that they hardly suspended their efforts.

The text of the *Plan of Chicago* makes its recommendations with assurance. The planners' internal correspondence nevertheless reveals that there was a great deal of discussion, and sometimes even disagreement, on the way to put these recommendations in their final form. The planners also considered and dropped some startling ideas. One such notion was to move City Hall a block west of where it was then (and is still) located and to build a plaza between it and the County Building, rather than (as is the case) combine them in one structure. Another called for diverting the South Branch of the Chicago River about fifteen blocks and almost two miles west to Ashland Avenue in order to encourage expansion of the downtown in this direction. The evolution of three sets of proposals is of particular interest in understanding the work of the planners: their recommendations for Michigan Avenue, for the mouth of the Chicago River and the nearby lakefront, and for railway terminals.

The Michigan Avenue proposal involved a plan to widen and elevate that street for several blocks above and below the Main Branch of the Chicago River and to connect the north and south segments with a double-level bridge. This would transform Michigan Avenue into a continuous boulevard linking the North and South sides. The Chicago River and lakefront discussion considered whether and how much to devote the shoreline near where the river met the lake to harbor facilities for Great Lakes commercial shipping. In regard to the railway terminals, the planners hoped to reduce inefficiency and congestion by keeping freight passing through Chicago out of the downtown and by reorganizing the placement of passenger stations in the heart of the city.

What was called the "Boulevard to Connect the North and South Sides" was the first substantive matter the planners pondered at length and for which they set up a special subcommittee. They may have made it a priority as a preemptive move, since Burnham advised them that other groups in the city were currently discussing the same topic. The idea of making Michigan Avenue south of the Main Branch of the Chicago River and Pine Street to the north into one continuous boulevard had been under serious scrutiny for at least three years. This improvement struck many people as obvious and necessary, especially since the current easternmost bridge across the Main Branch, located at Rush Street, was a terrible bottleneck. According to the planners, elevating the street would both enable it to pass over the Chicago and Northwestern tracks north of the river and allow commercial enterprises and vehicles to conduct their business on a lower roadway while pleasure and retail traffic would move overhead, free of the presence of larger vehicles. Connecting Michigan Avenue and Pine Street was an extremely complicated proposition, however, and not only from a design and engineering standpoint. Implementation would require the approval of different authorities within the city, condemnation of property on the east side of the street south of the river and on the west side north of it, and appropriate legislation, not to mention winning popular support in a bond referendum.

The Commercial Club pulled out all the stops in support of its Michigan Avenue plan, spending several thousand dollars to hire a publicist and producing a special booklet devoted to this single improvement before the *Plan of Chicago* as a whole was published. As Burnham had anticipated, other groups proposed contrasting designs in the period the *Plan of Chicago* was being prepared. The Michigan Avenue Improvement Association, for example, called for a single-level bridge and for a boulevard only a hundred feet wide, issuing a pamphlet of its own that praised its plan as simple, aesthetically appealing, relatively inexpensive, and free of legal obstacles. Michigan Avenue was the main topic of the meeting with Mayor Busse, Aldermen Kenna and Coughlin, and other city officials in late October 1907.

For over two years, Burnham urged his colleagues to stick to the "ideal" scheme of widening the avenue as much as possible (which they calculated at 246 feet), elevating it to create two levels, and building a double-decker bridge across the river with plazas on both sides of the upper level. He wrote to Bennett from Europe about the text of the booklet, instructing him that it should point out as explicitly as possible to property owners in the area that the Commercial Club's proposal would raise the value of their holdings. "If the property owners are captured by the argument as it is, then well and good & our object is accomplished; if they are not, then the real estate argument must be used, raw," Burnham wrote. "For they are, as they have frankly said, fighting for their pockets," he went on, "and nothing but proof that this scheme will pay them very directly will have any weight with them."

The discussion of the future of the lakefront, which began shortly after the fair, intensified in the first decade of the twentieth century. This discussion focused not only on what to do with Grant Park, but also on whether maintaining and developing the shore as a public park would jeopardize the city's commercial well-being. As Governor Deneen was about to sign a bill passed in April 1907 that would authorize the construction of a shoreline parkway from Grant Park to Jackson Park, he received a letter from the most persistent opponent to this plan, Colonel W. H. Bixby, the United States Army engineer in charge of federal projects in the city. Bixby wanted to build a line of docks along the lakeshore north and south of Grant Park to serve lake-going ships. A few weeks later, Bixby wrote to Delano, "The future prosperity of Chicago is dependent upon an Outer Harbor," next to which other infrastructural improvements were "bagatelles and trifles." Early in 1908 Delano invited Bixby to lunch in Burnham's office with Burnham and the members of the General Committee and of the Committee on the Lake Front.

Bixby evidently based his view on the assumption that manufacturing and wholesale trade would continue to be located in or near the center of the city, making it important to afford ships access to this area. Whether or not he was correct, if his advice were followed, much of the downtown lakefront would be dominated by piers, railroad tracks, and warehouses. The Commercial Club responded quickly to Bixby's opposition. Norton wrote to club president John Farwell that several of his fellow planners agreed "that there is sufficient sentiment in favor of an outer harbor to make it imperative as a matter of tactics that we definitely state at this time that The Commercial Club will appoint a committee to investigate that question with Mr. Burnham." This was not entirely insincere, since Burnham and others had previously been given pause by suggestions that the city required an improved outer harbor for ships too large to use the river. In any case, they invited and received written commentary on the idea from several Chicagoans knowledgeable about Great Lakes trade.

Some of their correspondents agreed with Bixby, but the thinking that carried the day contended that the future of freight shipping lay with trains, not boats. Bennett and others also argued that Calumet Harbor provided a better commercial port than did the stretch of lakefront nearer the center of Chicago since it was possible to provide access from there for heavy industry, which was increasingly located on the city's Far South Side. In addition, concentrating large-scale shipping in Calumet Harbor would ease downtown traffic problems by reducing the number of times it would be necessary to open bridges across the Chicago River. And, of course, this would leave the lakefront closer to the river free for recreational development.

When Charles Norton wrote to hardware wholesaler Adolphus Bartlett in February 1907 about Bartlett's possible service on the Committee on Railway Terminals, Norton described the relocation of passenger stations as "the one greatest problem which confronts Mr. Burnham in preparing his Plan of Chicago." Moving terminals would affect some twenty competing private railroad companies. These changes would in turn necessitate a rearrangement of roads, streetcar lines, elevated trains, subways, and other elements of the urban infrastructure. But virtually everyone agreed that something had to be done. The planners' solution was to use their influence in the business community to get the top management of the different railroads to sit down together and talk directly to one another. They wrote to the heads of all the railroads doing business in Chicago, inviting them or designated representatives to a buffet lunch and full afternoon meeting to take place on July 14, 1908, in Burnham's office.

The minutes of this meeting reveal that Burnham and planning committee members told their guests that the purpose of the gathering was "to obtain a means of free communication" between the Committee on Railway Terminals and the railroads, with the purpose of "harmonious work to a common end, and the securing of a Plan which would have the co-operation and approval of the railroads." The planners presented their ideas on what to do about rail congestion and inefficiency and then left their visitors to discuss matters among themselves. At the close of this discussion, the railroad executives thanked their hosts and then enigmatically stated that they desired to assure the committee "that we intend to co-operate with you as far as we can—at least up to the point of a full discussion of what may or can be done and when we can do it." The issue remained unresolved and under discussion for years after the *Plan of Chicago* appeared.

Burnham had submitted a draft of the *Plan* early in the spring of 1908. On April 30, the General Committee passed a resolution accepting this document, declaring that Burnham had "fully and entirely fulfilled" the conditions under which he was hired and gratefully acknowledging his work. On Burnham's recommendation, the planners asked his former Washington plan associate Charles Moore, now an executive for a trust company in Detroit, to assume the responsibility of completing the writing and editing of the *Plan of Chicago*. Moore's fee was $2,000 plus expenses. Burnham continued to attend and host meetings, and he spoke and wrote in support of the *Plan* until his death four years after the resolution of thanks.

FIGURE 33. Jules Guerin, as pictured in 1924. Northwestern University Library.

Several months before Burnham completed his draft, he and Bennett had secured the services of a group of seven gifted artists to prepare the drawings that would accompany the text. Burnham was convinced that making the *Plan of Chicago*'s ideas visually compelling and seductive was vital to winning Chicagoans over to its proposals. Jules Guerin (as his name appears in the *Plan,* though in his correspondence with Burnham he signed it Guérin) and Fernand Janin were the most significant illustrators. Guerin, born in St. Louis in 1866, was a painter, illustrator, and muralist who had done some of the renderings for the Washington plan. His work graced the pages of leading magazines and, in the years to come, Pennsylvania Station in New York, the 1915 Panama-Pacific International Exposition in San Francisco, and the Lincoln Memorial in Washington. His depiction of the parade scene from *Aïda* on the decorative fire curtain of the Civic Opera House (1929)—done in a striking combination of rose, pink, olive, gold, and bronze—pleases Chicago audiences to this day. Bennett evidently knew the Parisian Janin, who executed the major elevation and perspective drawings, from his student days at the École des Beaux-Arts. Janin was only in his late twenties when he worked on the *Plan*.

The planners entrusted publication to the Lakeside Press of Commercial Club member Thomas Donnelley, who supervised the production. They had originally projected an edition of 1,000 copies, but they raised this to 1,650, including 100 ordered by Burnham and 50 by Norton. They decided to issue this volume as one might publish a fine art book, in what one member called a "deluxe limited special edition" with an individual number assigned to each copy. This would reward subscribers and impress readers. Bennett created a Commercial Club cipher for the cover. The originally scheduled date of publication, set perhaps unrealistically early for such an elaborate book, was pushed back a few times. On January 28, 1909, the planners met to discuss the proofs of the first six chapters. On March 14, they blessed the entire text with their approval. Finally, on July 4, the *Plan of Chicago* was ready for all the world to see.

CHAPTER SIX

READING THE PLAN

The *Plan of Chicago* is a groundbreaking document, the product of its several creators' thinking about Chicago and urban planning and also about how to present an alternative view of modern urban life as cogently as possible. It reads like an extended version of one of Burnham's speeches, which mix uplifting exhortations and abstract principles with hard numbers and tight logic.

In its eighth and last chapter, the *Plan* provides a useful six-point summary of its key recommendations:

1. "The improvement of the Lake Front," notably the building of a shoreline parkway and the development of Grant Park, as Burnham had advocated since the mid-1890s;

2. "The creation of a system of highways outside the city" in the form of concentric semicircular roadways, the outermost of which would loop from southeast Wisconsin around to northwest Indiana;

3. "The improvement of railway terminals," mainly by locating them along Canal and Twelfth streets at the edges of the current downtown, and "the development of a complete traction system for both freight and passengers," consisting of trains, tunnels, elevated rapid transit, and subways that would enable freight shipped through Chicago to bypass the center of the city and make the arrival and departure of passengers in this area more efficient and convenient;

4. "The acquisition of an outer park system, and of parkway circuits," continuing the work the Outer Belt Commission began in 1903;

5. "The systematic arrangement of the streets and avenues within the city," including the cutting of new diagonal streets and the widening of important thoroughfares, "in order to facilitate the movement to and from the business district";

6. "The development of centers of intellectual life and of civic administration, so related as to give coherence and unity to the city," notably by building new homes for the Field Museum and Crerar Library near the Art Institute in Grant Park, and by constructing a mammoth civic center of government buildings at the intersection of widened Congress and Halsted streets. (The Crerar Library, privately endowed but open to the public, was established in 1897. At the time of the *Plan,* it was located in the Marshall Field building.)

Following the last chapter of the *Plan* is an appendix, "Legal Aspects of the Plan of Chicago," prepared by attorney and Commercial Club member Walter L. Fisher, former president of the Chicago Municipal Voters League and future secretary of the interior under President Taft. It details which of the *Plan's* recommendations could be carried out under existing legislation and which required legal changes, especially in regulations regarding the city's power to appropriate private property. Fisher advised that many of the *Plan's* proposals were possible within current laws and that the legislature could readily approve several other recommendations. He observed that the *Plan's* most ambitious ideas would require additional authority, the most important being the right to exceed current debt limits in issuing bonds.

To reduce the *Plan of Chicago* to a list of points risks overlooking the luxurious experience of reading such a lavish volume and also of missing what it is really saying, that is, what underlying conceptions about Chicago it presents. As carefully thought out as it is, the *Plan of Chicago* makes its first appeal to the senses, not the mind. Like many of D. H. Burnham and Company's buildings, it exudes a forthright and foursquare gravitas. This is literally true, since it measures twelve and a half inches high, ten inches wide, an inch and three-quarters thick, and it weighs in at over five pounds. With its midnight green cover, into which the title and the ornate cipher of the Commercial Club are impressed in gold, and its cream-colored pages, gilded on the top and rough trimmed at the edges, the *Plan of Chicago* is not a mere book but a tome, whose proper pedestal is a mahogany boardroom table tastefully polished to a rich sheen. It presents itself as something to be admired as much as understood.

This impression continues once one reverently opens the *Plan*. An elegant note in the front matter informs the fortunate reader which

FIGURE 34. The *Plan of Chicago*, with the cipher of the Commercial Club designed by Bennett. This copy is in the Charles Deering McCormick Library of Special Collections, Northwestern University. Stefani Foster, Academic Technologies, Northwestern University.

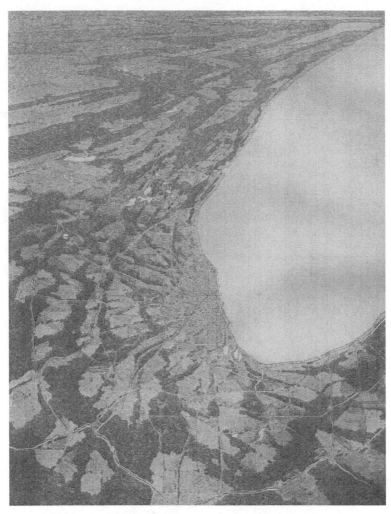

FIGURE 35. Guerin's drawing, which faces the title page, introduces the reader to the pastel palette he uses throughout the *Plan of Chicago* to create the alternate world of the Chicago that might be. Chicago Historical Society (ICHi-39070_1e).

of the limited edition of 1,650 copies he or she has the honor to hold. Opposite the title page is the first of Guerin's renderings. While the subject of this illustration is immediately identifiable as a bird's-eye view of the southwest reaches of Lake Michigan meeting the settled prairie, the vantage required to see the enormous expanse on display is so celestially high that the curvature of the earth is visible. Land and water strike the eye less as physical features than as epic masses. The title page conveys a sober momentousness. The three years over which the *Plan* was prepared, as well as the date of publication, are solemnly announced in Roman numerals. Though it speaks of the future, the volume presents itself as a monument.

Given the *Plan*'s portentous presence, one's first impulse is not to settle in and see what it has to say, but to leaf respectfully through its disciplined gorgeousness, focusing first on the dozens of illustrations that dominate the 124 pages of the main text. In so doing, the viewer—not yet quite the reader—enters a kind of alternate world. As noted,

FIGURE 36. The title page of the *Plan of Chicago*. Chicago Historical Society (ICHi-39070_1f).

there are very few views in the *Plan* of contemporary Chicago. The illustrations instead invite us to lose ourselves in wonder at the Chicago the planners dare us to imagine. Janin's hushed black-and-tan elevation of the Civic Center folds out to reveal a vision of an ideal neoclassical cityscape dominated by an elongated dome forty or more stories high that dwarfs the other dignified structures supporting and surrounding it. Guerin's skill with a limited but expressive range of color—mainly from pastel beiges and blues to deep violet and brown—and with perspective leads us into a more serenely civilized place than we have ever known.

Even once one sits down to absorb the import of the words that occupy the spaces between the illustrations, the *Plan* takes its time in getting to its ostensible subject. The presentation of specific proposals does not begin until the third chapter. The first two chapters prepare the reader's mind by explaining why planning is necessary and then describing in broad strokes what effective planning means. The opening chapter, "Origin of the Plan of Chicago," traces the steps leading up to the *Plan,* from the Columbian Exposition to the Commercial Club's decision to conduct a study that would suggest improvements in "the physical conditions of Chicago as they now exist." The second chapter, "City Planning in Ancient and Modern Times," highlights the traditions to which the *Plan* is heir, celebrating Paris as the planned city par excellence. Finally, in the next five chapters, the proposals arrive. They appear in a general geographical progression from the periphery of Chicago to its center: encircling highways, parks, transportation systems, and downtown. The book concludes with a discussion of the Civic Center, which the text deems, in an architectural metaphor, "the keystone of the arch" that is the *Plan*.

To look for a strictly logical order in the *Plan of Chicago* can be misleading and disappointing, however. Its proposals are not always laid out systematically, the prose is redundant in places, and while the chapters frequently provide much information, it sometimes is a little hard to grasp exactly what the *Plan* is recommending. In addition, although the book is without question finely produced, sharpness of detail is not a priority in the *Plan*'s images. Even the photographs

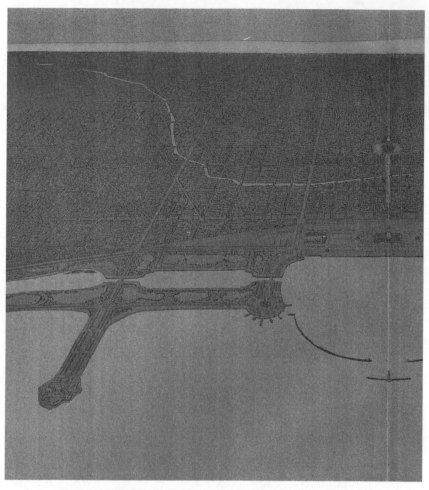

FIGURE 37. Jules Guerin is credited by name with a dozen illustrations in the *Plan*, including eleven architectural renderings and one sunny scene along Michigan Avenue. More than the work of any other of the several illustrators, Guerin's drawings give the *Plan* its distinctive visual character. The full title of this plate is "Chicago. View looking west over the city, showing the proposed Civic Center, the Grand Axis, Grant Park, and the Harbor." Chicago Historical Society (ICHI-39070_5s).

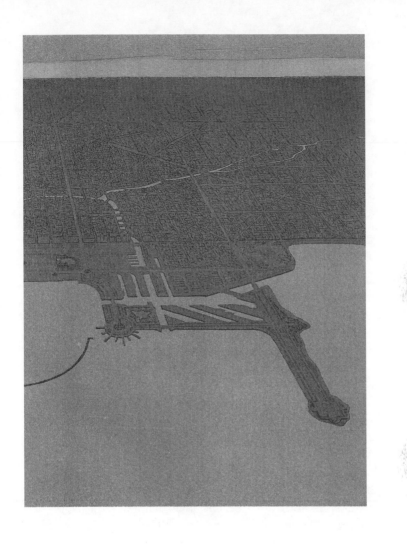

seem impressionistic rather than documentary, and the illustrations are suggestive rather than definitive. While they are carefully drawn and in several cases accompanied by explanatory legends, they are often difficult to decipher, however much they engage the eye. The text does not help much, since it rarely refers to the images. An exception is the brief mention of the dome of the Civic Center, but even here the *Plan* insists that it "does not seek to impose any particular form on structures." In another place, when the *Plan* is talking about transportation, it states that it is just picking some logical and natural routes. The planners would leave it up to engineers and other experts to determine the optimum location for this or that improvement. They would trust architectural schools and societies to come up with designs.

This odd element of diffidence in such a bold and ambitious document perhaps blunts the common criticism that the *Plan*'s authors—or at least the illustrators—seem to ignore or reject Chicago's place in the forefront of modern architecture, established in significant part by the many large and distinctive commercial and public buildings designed by Burnham and Root or D. H. Burnham and Company. Guerin often replaces Chicago's actual variegated cityscape with block upon block of uniform structures.

The criticism is very well taken, though the intention behind much of the *Plan*'s imagery seems to be to enlist the reader in a cause, not to offer faithful depictions of contemporary Chicago or precise blueprints of what might replace it. It is extremely unlikely that the planners wished to tear down the buildings that Burnham and other leading Chicago architects had designed, though they would have been happy to remove many others. The broader aim of the *Plan,* including Guerin's drawings, is to render its readers receptive to the notion that Chicago might in fact be made a place more beautiful and fine than anyone previously thought possible if they would only embrace the vision the *Plan* advances.

Of what does this vision consist? The specific recommendations the *Plan* offers are based on a set of governing ideas. The foundational assumption is at once the most optimistic and audacious. The planners above all believed in the malleability of history in general and of urban experience in particular. More specifically, they had faith in the ability of a self-appointed elite like themselves to re-create urban space and, as a result, expand the human prospect within that space. In the *Plan* they present themselves in terms characteristic of many turn-of-the-century reformers, not as a selfish special interest or as idle dreamers, but as "disinterested men of wide experience" who are indisputably well qualified to produce something good enough to "commend itself to the progressive spirit of the times." They confidently maintain that the *Plan* "conceals no private purpose, no hidden ends," but a "determination to bring about the very best conditions of city life for all the people."

Part of this determination involved convincing others that what some might consider irreconcilable goals were in fact mutually reinforcing objectives. As Paris proves, the *Plan* argues, a modern urban center like Chicago could possess convenience, functionality, beauty, and even dignity—a term it employs several times. The *Plan* admits that its proposals might seem unrealistic to skeptics, but it insists that they are practical. When the planners advocate rationalizing the location of railway passenger terminals and freight transfer depots and reducing water and air pollution, for example, they declare that bringing order and convenience to Chicago would be neither impossible nor even expensive. But "haphazard and ill-considered projects," not to mention dirt, would be terribly costly since they threaten human health and drive both working people and the wealthy away. Creating order and turning a profit are congruent rather than conflicting aims. In regard to rearranging transportation in the city, the planners state, "With things as they should be, every business man in Chicago would make more money than he does now."

The *Plan* employs both mechanistic and organic figures of speech to describe the better Chicago it promotes. On the one hand, the *Plan* declares that it is possible to make the city what it calls "an efficient instrument for providing all its people with the best possible conditions of living." On the other hand, it speaks of the downtown as "The Heart of Chicago," the title of chapter 7. The text retains this capitalization in subsequent uses of this term. The heart metaphor implies that Chicago has a life force that derives from and emanates

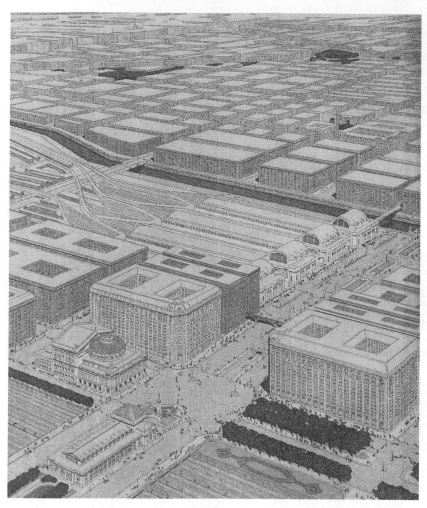

FIGURE 38. Illustrations like this one, which convey a vision of a downtown consisting of monumental buildings and a rigidly uniform cityscape, have drawn the criticism that the *Plan* neglects the needs of humane urban living. Chicago Historical Society (ICHi-39070_7b).

through the setting and the people who live there. Reflecting on the natural features that define the Chicago region, the *Plan* implies that the sheer scale of the lake and prairie places upon local residents the obligation of greatness. In less fortunately endowed places, "man and his works may be taken as the measure," but in Chicago "the city appears at that portion of illimitable space now occupied by a population capable of indefinite expansion." The metaphor also expresses the *Plan*'s contention that it is important to think regionally on at least two levels: first, by understanding the natural relationship between Chicago and the hinterland beyond; and, second, by keeping in mind the vital connection between the downtown and other parts of the city.

Chicagoans had to confront the current challenges they faced, the *Plan* tells them, by mustering their political and financial support behind its proposals. The final chapter reminds the reader that two short generations ago the city was barely a village. Since that time it had filled in its muddy streets, fashioned a park system, mounted a world's fair, and reversed the flow of the river. All of these were both practical and aesthetic achievements. Similarly, while the planners' proposals might seem to stretch the financial resources of Chicago, they in fact would take economic advantage of the city's existing natural and man-made features. Besides, these proposals could be realized without seriously increasing the existing tax burden, since the growth that they assured would bolster credit, lift assessed values, and stimulate the production of yet more wealth.

What was now required, the *Plan* states, was that the city's responsible elite lead the campaign for change. In the section of the sixth chapter that discusses the lake and prairie as defining Chicago as a place without limits, the *Plan of Chicago* comes closest to the rhetoric of the famous dictum attributed (though never definitively) to Burnham, "Make no little plans." It announces:

At no period in its history has the city looked far enough ahead. The mistakes of the past should be warnings for the future. There can be no reasonable fear lest any plans that may be adopted shall prove too broad and comprehensive. That idea may be dismissed as unworthy of a moment's consideration. Rather let it be understood that the broadest plans which the city can be brought to adopt to-day must prove inadequate and limited before the end of the next quarter of a century. The mind of man, at least as expressed in works he actually undertakes, finds itself unable to rise to the full comprehension of the needs of a city growing at the rate now assured for Chicago. Therefore, no one should hesitate to commit himself to the largest and most comprehensive undertaking; because before any particular plan can be carried out, a still larger conception will begin to dawn, and even greater necessities will develop.

While the *Plan of Chicago* is almost relentlessly upbeat, some passages do express warnings and doubts about urban life, especially if the proposals advanced by Burnham and the Commercial Club did not win support. Like the *Plan* as a whole, such passages appealed primarily to businessmen who had much at stake in Chicago's future. The closing words of the second chapter remind readers that the experience of other cities ancient and modern, abroad and in the United States, "teaches Chicago that the way to true greatness and continued prosperity" depends on keeping the city convenient, healthful, beautiful, and orderly. "The cities that truly exercise dominion rule by reason of their appeal to the highest emotions of the human mind," the *Plan* declares. This assertion is posed not by way of inspiration, but as a "problem" Chicago must solve.

A few pages later, the *Plan* puts specific blame behind the general charge that the same lack of regulation that perhaps once encouraged growth was now stifling Chicago. It takes to task the "speculative real estate agent" and "the speculative builder," who shortsightedly spread blight by trying to squeeze the last cent of profit out of every investment. In "The Heart of Chicago" chapter, the *Plan* discusses the need not only for widening Halsted Street but also for sanitary reform of industry and housing situated near Halsted's intersection with Chicago Avenue, an area that was beset by smoke, soot, pollution, and filth from trains, tanneries, garbage dumps, and coal docks. The *Plan* anticipates one of the more unfortunate methods of post–World War II urban renewal when it recommends cutting broad thoroughfares through "this unwholesome district" as a way to improve it. It also recommends, more ominously, "the remorseless enforcement

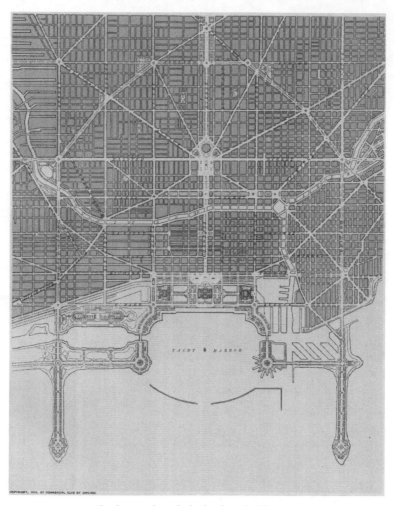

COPYRIGHT, 1909, BY COMMERCIAL CLUB OF CHICAGO

YACHT HARBOR

FIGURE 39. This diagram elegantly displays how the *Plan* proposed to arrange streets (including wide diagonal and radial boulevards and arteries), railways, parks, piers, harbors, and a civic center in a way that would present the city "as a complete organism in which all its functions are related one to another in such a manner that it will become a unit." Chicago Historical Society (ICHi-39070_6r).

of sanitary regulations" that would guarantee airier, brighter, and cleaner buildings.

The *Plan* implicitly condemns here what it sees as the dangerous excesses of capitalism, a system with which the Commercial Club was certainly allied. The *Plan* speaks with surprising directness of the city's need and right to place limits on speculators and landowners. It does so not only when it states that the lakefront "by right belongs to the people," but also when it defends the public appropriation of real estate needed to widen streets and to eradicate threats to sanitation and health. "It is no attack on private property," the *Plan* contends, "to argue that society has the inherent right to protect itself against abuses." If society does not exercise this right, the planners warned, it might be necessary to resort to socialism in some form. Chicago, unlike London, had not yet reached the point at which the city must intervene and provide housing for people living in unacceptable conditions. Unless timely action was taken, however, the *Plan* predicts that "such a course will be required in common justice to men and women so degraded by long life in the slums that they have lost all power of caring for themselves."

There are moments when the *Plan* even raises the possibility that city life is by its nature degrading to all people, not just the helplessly impoverished. Wage earners and even the well-to-do need access to parks because "density of population beyond a certain point results in disorder, vice, and disease, and thereby becomes the greatest menace to the well-being of the city itself." "Natural scenery," on the other hand, "furnishes the contrasting element to the artificiality of the city," a refuge "where mind and body are restored to a normal condition, and we are enabled to take up the burden of life in our crowded streets and endless stretches of buildings with renewed vigor and hopefulness." These remarks perhaps reflect the influence of Frederick Law Olmsted on Daniel Burnham, and they recall the anti-urban sentiment behind Burnham's decision to raise his children outside of Chicago, by the woods and lake in bucolic Evanston. "He who habitually comes in close contact with nature," the *Plan* observes, "develops saner methods of thought than can be the case when one is habitually shut up within the walls of a city."

The discussions of slums and parks state the planners' belief that a person's surroundings significantly determine his or her behavior. Time and again, the *Plan* maintains that terrible living conditions diminish the individual and, by extension, the entire city, and so should be of concern to the prosperous as well as the less fortunate. It speaks of the slums on the Near West Side as a "cosmopolitan district inhabited by a mixture of races living amid surroundings which are a menace to the moral and physical health of the community." There is as much alarm as sympathy in such passages. At times the *Plan* seems to advocate, as some reformers did, removing poor city children from their squalid home life and, by implication, from the negative influence of their parents, to places where they could be taught higher morals and values, that is, the standards by which middle- and upper-class Chicagoans presumably lived. It advocates constructing attractive public school buildings and playgrounds, so that "during all the year the school premises shall be the children's center, to which each child will become attached by those ties of remembrance that are restraining influences throughout life."

Such passages reflect the authors' view that one of the many purposes of city planning was control of the urban masses. While the *Plan of Chicago*'s central theme is how best to deal with rapid change in one of the most dynamic cities in the world, it is a remarkably conservative document that hopes to infuse in the public at large a belief in the status quo, in the social and economic hierarchy in which the planners were at the top. To give Burnham, Bennett, and the Commercial Club due credit, they were sincere in their civic-mindedness. They backed their rhetoric with their time and their money, serving on the boards of any number of charitable and social services agencies. Whatever their own blind spots, they were generous in their instincts and critical of the selfishness of some of their peers, realizing that any plan worth the name had to deal with the needs of the entire population.

At its most idealistic, the *Plan* tries to conceptualize just how that population could truly be a coherent urban community. The talk of the slums being a "cosmopolitan district inhabited by a mixture of races," as well as the comment made on the *Plan*'s very first page that the chaos of rapid growth was complicated by "the influx of people of many nationalities without common traditions or habits of life," indicates that the native-born Protestant men of the Commercial Club worried about the difficulty of finding common ground in Chicago, especially on their terms. They hoped that their *Plan* would unify Chicagoans by inspiring a civic pride and loyalty in an urban society that provided health, prosperity, and happiness to all those fortunate enough to dwell there.

It is no wonder, then, that the *Plan* saves its discussion of the "Heart of Chicago" for chapter 7, the last one that describes particular recommendations. The argument that it advances here for making Congress Street "a thoroughfare which would be to the city what the backbone is to the body" reveals a simultaneously hopeful and desperate desire for stability in unstable Chicago: "Thus, and thus only, is it possible to establish organic unity, and, in connection with the improvements of the streets above mentioned, to give order and coherence to the plan of Chicago." The Civic Center, as the *Plan* conceives it, would be comparable in its effect on Chicago to that of St. Peter's or the Forum on Rome, the Acropolis on Athens, or the Piazza San Marco on Venice. It would be, that is, "the very embodiment of civic life." If the *Plan of Chicago*'s proposals are realized, its authors promise, "the Lake front will be opened to those who are now shut away from it by lack of adequate approaches; the great masses of people which daily converge in the now congested center will be able to come and go quickly and without discomfort; the intellectual life of the city will be stimulated by institutions grouped in Grant Park; and in the center of all the varied activities of Chicago will rise the towering dome of the Civic Center, vivifying and unifying the entire composition."

The collective creation and joint authorship of the *Plan of Chicago* raise the intriguing question of precisely whose ideas and words it contains. The title page states that the *Plan* was "prepared under the direction of the Commercial Club" by Daniel H. Burnham and Edward H. Bennett, and that it was edited by Charles Moore. This is

FIGURE 40.   Fernand Janin's masterful elevation of the monumental
Civic Center. Chicago Historical Society (ICHI-39070_7p).

certainly true, in that Burnham and Bennett defined what the *Plan*
would discuss, members of the Commercial Club who served on the
various committees helped develop the content, and, at Burnham's recommendation, the club hired Moore in the spring of 1908 to edit the
draft written by Burnham. But this breakdown of the division of labor
is not very exact in explaining just who wrote what parts of the *Plan*.

Historian of architecture Kristen Schaffer has conducted the most
careful examination of the *Plan of Chicago*'s authorship, and she has
published some of her findings in her introduction to the Princeton
Architectural Press 1993 facsimile edition. While Schaffer sees the
final version of the *Plan* as reflecting the collective effort behind it,
she maintains that it unquestionably bears the mark of Burnham's
"genius." This "genius," she explains, "lies in his vision and his energy, in his ability to see how all the elements of the city and its func-
tioning are related and his tenacity in making others see it as well."
Schaffer's view squares with that of Charles Moore. In his biography

of Burnham, Moore says of the *Plan*, "The text, prepared from comprehensive notes made by [Burnham], is replete with his striking phrases, his happy characterizations, and is imbued with his settled philosophy: that the chief end of life is service to mankind in making life better and richer for every citizen." Despite his warm praise, Moore perhaps shortchanges Burnham somewhat in calling the draft, which consists of about three hundred handwritten pages, "comprehensive notes." As Schaffer describes it, the first half of this manuscript is the basis of many major elements of the final version of the *Plan*. Schaffer characterizes the second half of the manuscript as a more "technical" discussion of "the provision of services," such as utilities, education, and hospitals.

Comparing the draft not only with the published version but also with many other documents produced in the planning process, Schaffer reaches several noteworthy conclusions. Some of Burnham's "technical discussion" finds its way into the *Plan* in altered form, as what Schaffer calls "small asides." Schaffer states that a 1908 report prepared by the Committee on Interurban Roadways is the major source for the *Plan*'s discussion of that topic in chapter 3, while the section of chapter 7 on Michigan Avenue derives from the booklet on the subject by the Committee on Streets and Boulevards, which was published before the *Plan* appeared. Elsewhere Schaffer offers evidence that in writing his draft Burnham integrated material provided by Bennett, and that Moore borrowed from Burnham's speeches and addresses as part of the editing process.

Schaffer finds intriguing those sections of the Burnham manuscript that are "entirely omitted from the final version, or so reduced as to be effectively nullified." She persuasively argues that they "show a very different side of Burnham and challenge conventionally held assessments of the *Plan*" as socially conservative and apparently little concerned with the needs of ordinary citizens. The omitted sections, she contends, reveal a Burnham who believed more fully than the *Plan* would suggest in the need for the city government to take an active role in improving the living and working conditions of the mass of Chicagoans. Burnham also speaks in a way that the *Plan* does not of the importance of government enforcing the obligation of public utilities to serve the community responsibly. He similarly urges the authorities to see that hospitals do a better job of reducing human suffering, and that medical research benefits the common good, not just private medical schools and their staffs.

In addition, Burnham states that schoolhouses must be located nearer to the students who attend them and should be constructed with the health and safety of these students utmost in mind, and he provides details on how to accomplish this. Elsewhere in the manuscript, he advocates providing care centers for the children of working parents. While he speaks of the importance of developing a loyal and obedient citizenry, Burnham also expresses concern about the methods of those in power, recommending in language that seems remarkably modern that the police conduct their work in full view of the public lest they abuse their authority. Schaffer asserts that while some of Burnham's statements about the need of the city to provide for the well-being of its citizens are in the final version of the *Plan,* "had the draft version been published, the *Plan of Chicago* would hold a very different position in the history of city planning."

A close look at the archival material offers additional insights into the evolution of the *Plan* from draft report to published volume. Moore began his work by preparing an outline that he changed considerably as he proceeded toward the printed version. Chapter 1 in the outline does not include the narrative of how the *Plan* came to be written that appears in print. The outline also culminates with the intriguing topic "The City developing a soul." While the *Plan* talks about a city having other human qualities, including "spirit," "soul" is not one of them. More significantly, Moore changed the order of the presentation of topics, and he trimmed the historical background.

As for more precise editing, it is interesting to compare particular passages. Such a comparison reveals that Moore was an active editor who reworked much of Burnham's writing even as he left its meaning intact. A good example involves the similarities and differences between the first chapter of the *Plan* and related passages in the Burnham manuscript. A manuscript page on which Burnham has written "For Chap I" begins with a sentence that appears verbatim on page 4 of the *Plan of Chicago*. From there the two versions diverge radically, though some of Burnham's sentences, much edited, find their way into other pages of the *Plan*. Burnham also prepared notes headed "History of Movement" that start with the World's Columbian Exposition and then explain how the Merchants Club decided to hire him. These resemble the narrative on pages 6 and 7 of the *Plan,* but there are multiple differences.

Some of Burnham's phrasing is more exuberantly florid than what appears in print. Of the fair, Burnham writes, "A lily springing from the rich soil of commerce! Commerce the art breeder!" He also is not always shy about acknowledging his own efforts, as when he writes, "Burnham took laboring oar at all the above meetings." Moore's language is generally more restrained, and he does not give Burnham or any of the Commercial Club planners such personal credit. Whether Moore acted on his own or at others' direction is unclear, though the planners reviewed and approved the galleys before publication.

Burnham certainly does not seem to have simply handed the manuscript off to Moore and then stepped away. On the top of a galley of the opening page is a handwritten note from Burnham to Bennett,

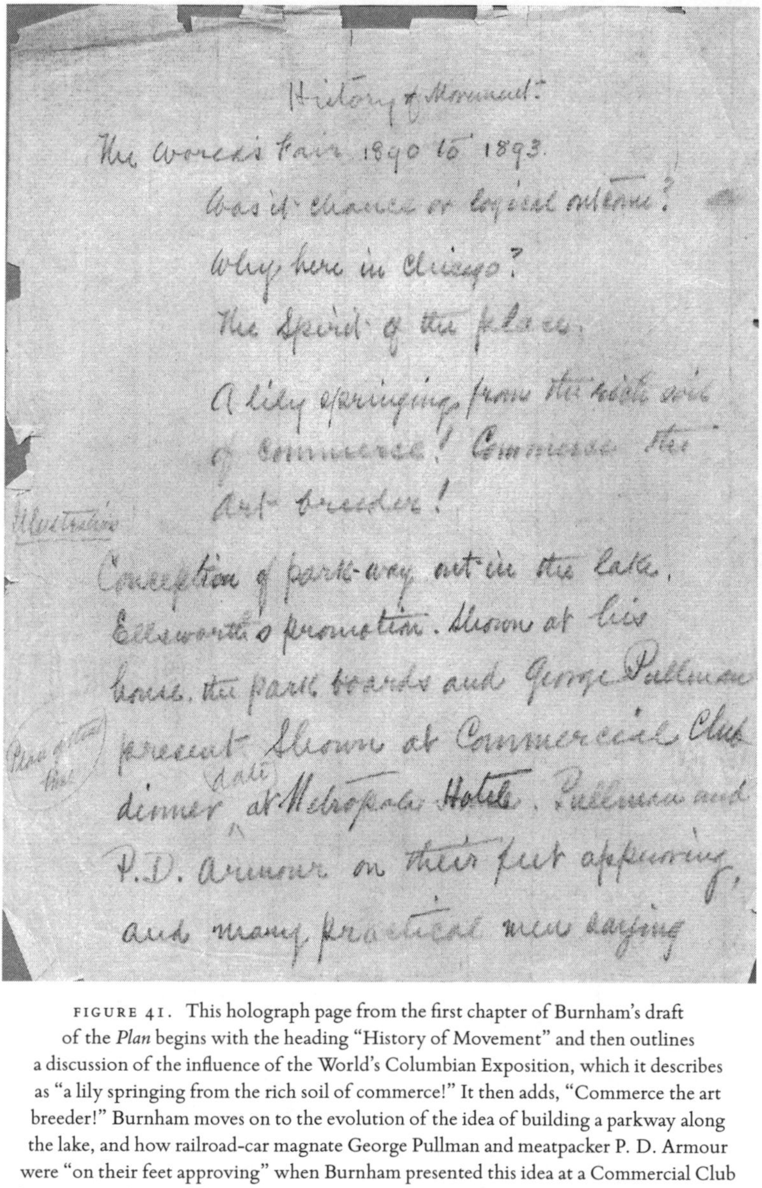

History of Movement.

The World's Fair 1890 to 1893.

Was it chance or logical outcome?

Why here in Chicago?

The Spirit of the place.

A lily springing from the rich soil of commerce! Commerce the Art breeder!

Illustrations

Conception of park-way out in the lake. Ellsworth's promotion. Shown at his house. the park boards and George Pullman present. Shown at Commercial Club dinner (date) at Metropole Hotel. Pullman and P. D. Armour on their feet approving, and many practical men saying

FIGURE 41. This holograph page from the first chapter of Burnham's draft of the *Plan* begins with the heading "History of Movement" and then outlines a discussion of the influence of the World's Columbian Exposition, which it describes as "a lily springing from the rich soil of commerce!" It then adds, "Commerce the art breeder!" Burnham moves on to the evolution of the idea of building a parkway along the lake, and how railroad-car magnate George Pullman and meatpacker P. D. Armour were "on their feet approving" when Burnham presented this idea at a Commercial Club dinner. Daniel H. Burnham Collection, Ryerson and Burnham Archives, The Art Institute of Chicago. Reproduction © The Art Institute of Chicago.

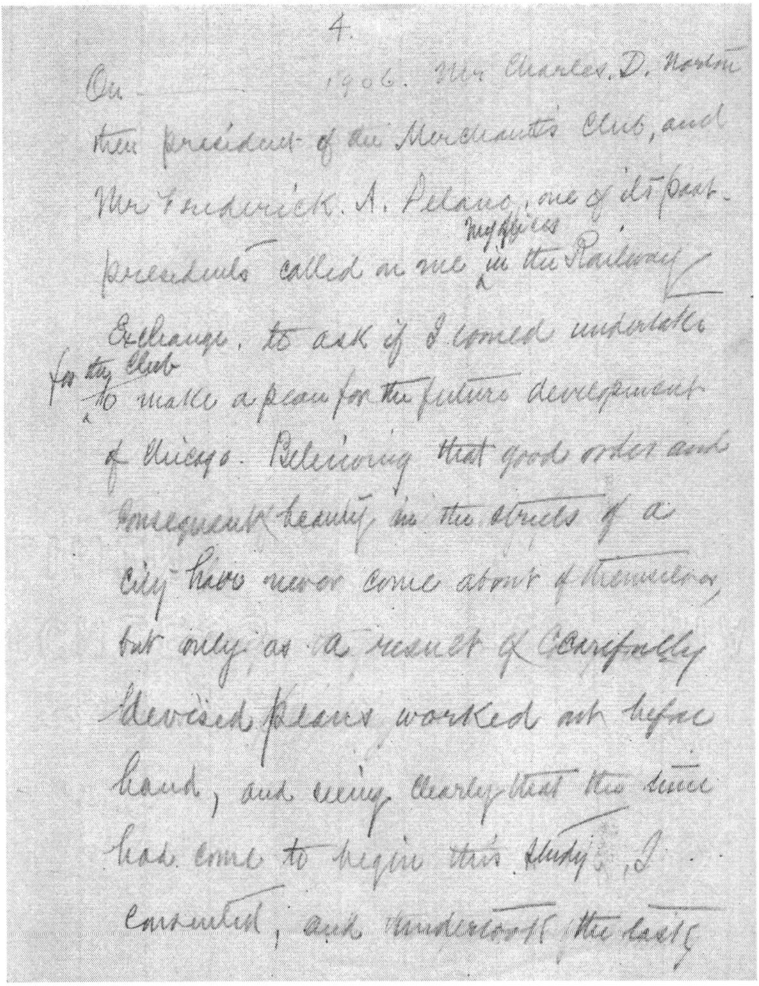

4.

[handwritten manuscript page, partially legible]

On _____ 1906. Mr Charles D. Norton, then president of the Merchants Club, and Mr Frederick A. Delano, one of its past-presidents called on me in the Railway Exchange, to ask if I would undertake to make a plan for the future development of Chicago. Believing that good order and consequent beauty in the streets of a city have never come about of themselves, but only as a result of carefully devised plans worked out before hand, and seeing clearly that the time had come to begin this study, I consented, and undertook the task

FIGURE 42. On this page Burnham recalls how Charles Norton and Frederick Delano invited him to prepare what became the *Plan of Chicago*. "Believing that good order and consequent beauty in the streets of a city have never come about of themselves, but only as a result of carefully devised plans worked out before hand, and seeing clearly that the time had come to begin this study, I consented," Burnham writes. Burnham's first-person narration of how he came to work on the *Plan* is not in the final version, but his belief in the value of "good order" and the need for careful and determined planning to achieve it is behind every page. Daniel H. Burnham Collection, Ryerson and Burnham Archives, The Art Institute of Chicago. Reproduction © The Art Institute of Chicago.

which reads, "Mr. Bennett: I want this paper at the meeting with Mr. Moore. DHB." Someone, presumably Burnham, suggested changes in the chapter title, which was further altered before publication. On the bottom right of the page is a notation for the printer in Moore's handwriting. All of these marks are indications of a complex collaboration.

CHAPTER SEVEN

PROMOTION

Handsomely produced and lavishly illustrated, the *Plan of Chicago* was its own best advertisement. But the men who created the *Plan* had no intention of limiting their labors only to preparing and publishing the *Plan,* as massive an effort as that was. They never assumed that the people of Chicago, without considerable additional urging, would immediately comprehend and approve of the *Plan*'s proposals and then rush to implement them. The planners also knew that the meetings they held with various groups and individuals as the *Plan* was being developed, and the limited edition of copies of the *Plan* they printed, reached only a very small if influential segment of the population. Even before they had formulated any specific recommendations for improving Chicago, they began a strategy for the figurative selling of whatever these recommendations might be to government officials, the business community at large, property owners, and voters. The *Plan* itself was forward-looking, but in some respects the publicity techniques the planners used to generate support, especially after its release, were even more innovative and modern.

The members of the planning committees made sure first of all that they maintained the interest and support of their core constituency, the subscribers who funded the *Plan of Chicago*. The *Plan* prominently acknowledges these people in its opening pages, where it lists the names of the fourteen businesses, one law firm, two estates, and 312 individuals (308 of them men, judging from their names) who contributed prior to June 1, 1909. The planners, who were virtually all among the listed contributors, had also been solicitous of the subscribers while work was in progress. In addition, they made sure that the general membership of the Commercial Club was well informed. On January 25, 1909, Burnham was the featured speaker at a closed meeting of the club at the Congress Hotel that was devoted to the *Plan*. He illustrated his talk that evening with scale models, carefully mounted drawings, and thirty-five lantern slides.

Burnham and the committee members discussed at length how to evoke the most positive public reception—and one likely to translate into action—once the *Plan of Chicago* appeared. As early as their third meeting, minutes of this meeting reveal, they had agreed "that a certain amount of money must be set aside to carry on a campaign of education on behalf of this Plan of Chicago, with lectures in Public Schools, etc., to show what was proposed in this matter here and had already been done in similar matters elsewhere." The question that occupied them the most at this point was how to deal with the press. Keeping up good relations with newspaper editors and reporters was particularly important because, in an age before radio and television, print was by far the public's major source of information. Since Chicago was served by a dozen daily newspapers that competed with each other for newsworthy stories and expressed different political outlooks, shaping opinion was a challenge.

The planners wished to maintain secrecy when it seemed advantageous to do so, but also to get ample and positive news coverage when that was useful. Among the matters agreed upon at their meeting of April 1, 1907, was that "a carefully prepared statement should be given out to the newspapers" at the end of April on planning progress, "not going into detail—and above all things—not using all of our ammunition at this time." Their inability to control either the timing or the content of coverage proved irritating to these businessmen, who were used to giving orders and having them followed. A week before Burnham was to describe the *Plan* to the Commercial Club membership, club secretary John Scott wrote to *Tribune* publisher and club member Joseph Medill McCormick. Scott requested that "the Closed Meeting on the 25th instant be given no publicity," pressuring McCormick by adding that "the members bespeak your courtesy in the matter."

McCormick said that as a member he was honor bound to treat the meeting as confidential, but that trying to squelch reporters and editors was another thing entirely. He advised *Plan of Chicago* General Committee chairman Charles Norton, "You know by this time that it is impossible to keep news out of all the papers and therefore out of any one of them." At McCormick's suggestion, Norton prepared a disingenuous announcement stating that nothing of great importance would happen at the meeting, and he brokered an agreement among the editors of leading papers that none would cover it and so no paper would scoop the others. Just in case, when the planners met on January 23 to make final preparations for the January 25 presentation to the membership, they authorized Burnham to hire security men to guard that no one would photograph the drawings on display.

The very fact that the Commercial Club attracted so much attention and believed it needed to take these precautions shows how powerful the press thought the club's members were. The planners, in turn, felt that the media's support was vital to their work. Members of the *Plan* committees went out of their way to acknowledge and encourage positive coverage. They sent a note to *Chicago Daily Chronicle* editor H. W. Seymour in the spring of 1907, for instance, expressing their "personal appreciation of your clear and readable [i.e., favorable] Editorial in this morning's Chronicle on the question of the North and South Connecting Boulevard." Later the same year, General Committee treasurer Walter H. Wilson shared a similarly laudatory editorial from the *Chicago American* with Norton, urging him to write to *American* editor Andrew Lawrence. "Ever since the bankers and 'certain portions of the administration' got [Lawrence] in line on the financial situation," Wilson explained, "we have been complimenting him to beat the band by daily telephones and letters, and I think it has done him a lot of good and opened his eyes as to what his paper might accomplish along the proper lines."

The proposal to turn Michigan Avenue into a boulevard connecting the North Side and the South Side proved to be the biggest publicity headache. Some property owners, business associations, and newspaper editorials criticized and ridiculed the club's proposals. Early in the planning process, even McCormick's *Tribune* said that a double-level boulevard was a bad idea since it lacked aesthetic appeal and was unlikely to function well. After reading the editorial, Norton wrote to Clyde Carr, chair of the Committee on Streets and Boulevards, instructing him to intervene before a majority of the city's newspapers adopted a negative view of the matter "from which they will find it difficult to retire." Norton asked Carr to direct Edward Bennett—Daniel Burnham was traveling in Europe—to make "a careful and attractive drawing of the ideal scheme" for the boulevard that very morning and to schedule appointments with twelve different newspaper editors in order to demonstrate to them the scheme's merits before they committed their papers to an opposing position.

This did not prevent some reporters and cartoonists from lampooning the idea of an elevated Michigan Avenue as "a boulevard on stilts." The planners told the Board of Local Improvements and anyone else who would listen that this characterization distorted the facts. Such opposition also led to their decision to publish their proposals for Michigan Avenue right away as a separate booklet and to hire *Tribune* reporter Henry Barrett Chamberlain (in some places his name was spelled Chamberlin) to work for them as a publicist. In addition, someone—possibly Burnham or Bennett—prepared a formal statement on the connecting boulevard, reminding Chicagoans that the planners had exhaustively considered all the other options for Michigan Avenue before arriving at their own recommendation. As part of this consideration, the statement explained, they had made scale models of these options. The statement invited members of the public to view the models and judge for themselves which proposal was best. It was not the planners' purpose, they claimed, "to attempt to dictate to the government or to the people of the City of Chicago."

The Commercial Club carefully staged the release of the *Plan of Chicago* on July 4, 1909, as a major event. A special Publication Committee, chaired by John Scott, met with Chamberlain and General Committee vice chairman Charles H. Wacker to discuss their strategy. Norton had by this time left Chicago for Washington and his

FIGURE 43. The cover cartoon of the November 1914 *North-West Side Monthly Bulletin*, titled "The Big Stick and the Hand That Wields It," depicts those most in favor of the boulevard and bridge as bloated, bejeweled, and beady-eyed "State Street Interests," who want to steal more business by opening a bridge between the downtown and the North Side. The stick they wield is the editorial policy of the daily newspapers. The pennant flying from the building on the right reads, "M.F. & Co.," naming the Marshall Field State Street store as a chief culprit. The *Bulletin* was published by the North-West Side Commercial Association. Edward H. Bennett Collection, Ryerson and Burnham Archives, The Art Institute of Chicago. Reproduction © The Art Institute of Chicago.

new job as assistant secretary of the treasury, so that Wacker was now in charge. Wacker and Scott spoke with the managing editors of the leading newspapers, including the foreign-language press, and obtained signed agreements from them to release the story on the *Plan of Chicago* in the afternoon editions of Saturday, July 3, and the morning editions on the Fourth of July. Three papers—the *Examiner,* the *Tribune,* and the *Record Herald*—published special illustrated supplements on the *Plan,* which the planners mailed to what the Publication Committee report called "a carefully selected list of one thousand names of persons in or nearby Chicago, whose interest is desired."

In May Burnham made arrangements with Commercial Club member and Art Institute of Chicago president Charles L. Hutchinson for an exhibition of the Guerin and Janin drawings in the Art Institute's first-floor northeast gallery. Burnham and Bennett supervised the details, from special lighting to the placement of vases and other props. The Publication Committee made sure the business community was given top priority in seeing the display. It issued three thousand free tickets to members of the Chicago Association of Commerce for a private viewing between July 5 and July 8. The committee distributed close to ten thousand more tickets to several additional clubs and associations. After leaving the Art Institute, the drawings traveled to other cities in America and Europe, including Philadelphia, Boston, London, and Düsseldorf. When there proved to be more requests to host this exhibition than the General Committee could accommodate, it offered to send sets of lantern slides.

The Publication Committee put Chamberlain in charge of distribution of the *Plan of Chicago.* He began with members of the Commercial Club and *Plan* subscribers, who received them for free. He also sent more than four hundred copies to aldermen and other city and county officials, park commissioners, Chicago members of the Illinois General Assembly, other state officeholders, United States congressmen, local and federal judges, the Sanitary District board, Chicago libraries and clubs, numerous magazines and newspapers, and President Taft and his cabinet. Some of the remaining copies were apparently sold for $25 each. This price was for all practical purposes out of the reach of most Chicagoans. The Commercial Club presented the ceremonial first copy, hand-bound in leather and with marbled paper insets, to Daniel Burnham.

The planners understood that if the *Plan* was to be implemented, they needed to have the support of Chicagoans who would vote on the referendums to authorize the bonds required to fund major improvements. Not trusting elected officials to take the initiative in selling the public on the *Plan,* the Commercial Club moved aggressively on three related fronts. The first was to obtain the city's formal approval of the *Plan of Chicago* as Chicago's official planning document. The second was to see to it that there was an organization actively pushing political leaders to put the *Plan* into action. The third was to convince the community as a whole of the value of the *Plan.* The effort to achieve these goals constituted one of the pioneering exercises in large-scale public relations.

Walter Wilson, who was at this time controller of the city of Chicago, took the first step toward the formal acceptance of the *Plan.* Speaking on behalf of Mayor Busse, Wilson issued a statement on July 4 praising the *Plan of Chicago*'s proposals as befitting Chicago's business character and "spirit of 'do.'" Two days later Busse himself commended the Commercial Club warmly and officially endorsed the *Plan.* As the planners desired, the city council empowered Busse to appoint a commission of elected officials and private citizens to consider the proposals and how to enact them. On November 1, Busse nominated and the council approved 328 men to serve on the Chicago Plan Commission, with Charles Wacker as chairman. The commission met for the first time on November 4 in the city council chamber, though half of its members were absent. Wacker's first act was to name twenty-six of their number to an executive committee "to undertake active work on a plan." Most of the Commercial Club members who participated in creating the *Plan* were on the larger commission, and several of them were on the executive committee as well.

On Saturday evening, January 8, 1910, the Commercial Club hosted the Chicago Plan Commission at a dinner at the Congress Hotel. Club president Theodore Robinson served as toastmaster, and Charles Norton returned from Washington to speak on "The Broader Aspects of City Planning." In his address, Norton was unapologetic about the

FIGURE 44. Charles H. Wacker, chairman of the Chicago Plan
Commission from 1909 to 1926. Northwestern University Library.

Plan's ambitions. What everyone had to realize, he explained, was
that the real question was not whether it was too big, but whether it
was big enough. "And when we reach that viewpoint," he continued,
"we shall discover how great was the vision and the genius of Burnham." In his remarks that evening, Wacker recapitulated the *Plan*'s
history, calling it "the best book on city planning ever published."
He assured his wealthy listeners that the increased prosperity produced by the *Plan*'s implementation would benefit poorer citizens
more than would devoting funds to housing or public services. When
it was his turn to speak, Alderman Bernard W. Snow—chairman of
the city council's Committee on Finance and an advocate of making
local government more efficient—agreed with Wacker's contention
that while the *Plan of Chicago* would cost millions to implement, this
would be a good investment. Snow noted, however, that the *Plan* was
not to be regarded "as anything more than a well-thought-out suggestion" that might be modified. But it was essential to get to work;

otherwise the *Plan* "will sleep the sleep of the forgotten in the dust-covered tomb of the years."

Snow's remarks signaled that the real promotional effort had only begun. Wacker understood this, and he drove the Commercial Club and the Chicago Plan Commission hard to assure that recommendations became realities. At the club's annual banquet in April, he announced that it had raised $20,000 to educate the public by means of lectures, widely circulated editions of the *Plan*'s contents, and other measures. Two weeks later the Chicago Plan Commission decided that it would use this money to "cover the town" with a publicity campaign of lantern-slide talks delivered in multiple languages wherever an audience could be gathered, whether in churches, schools, theaters, assembly halls, or private residences. The commission's aim, as the *Chicago Tribune* put it, was "to arouse interest in the efforts of the commission to make Chicago the 'most beautiful city in the world'" and to "imbue every man, woman, and child with the spirit of cooperation." The paper soon gave Wacker space in its pages to argue for the value of the *Plan* directly.

Wacker's most important move, however, was to hire Walter L. Moody to lead the publicity campaign. Moody could have been the protagonist in a Sinclair Lewis novel. Well known in the Chicago business community as the general manager of the Chicago Association of Commerce, he was the author of *Men Who Sell Things,* published the year before the *Plan*. Moody's book was a guide to selling based on his twenty years of experience as a "commercial ambassador," his term for a salesman, whom he saw as a benevolent servant not only of his employers but also of the public at large. Moody was in his mid-thirties when he went to work for the Chicago Plan Commission in the middle of 1910, and by 1911 he was its managing director. Eight years later he described the task of "selling" the *Plan of Chicago* in another book, titled *What of the City?* This 430-page volume is part personal memoir and part history of city planning, though it is mainly a public relations instructional manual.

Moody begins *What of the City?* with the admission that he himself is neither architect nor engineer. His profession involves the "scientific promotion" of city planning, which he calls "in all its practical

FIGURE 45. In this lantern slide of the proposed Civic Center, which was adapted from drawings in the *Plan,* the buildings are colored in an alluring if improbable deep blue. *Plan of Chicago,* plate 132. "View, looking west, of the proposed Civic Center plaza and buildings, showing it as the center of the system of arteries of circulation and of the surrounding country." Historic Architecture and Landscape Image Collection, Ryerson and Burnham Archives, The Art Institute of Chicago. Reproduction © The Art Institute of Chicago.

essentials . . . a work of promotion—salesmanship." And what does city planning require, above all? "Money," Moody explains, using small capitals for emphasis, continuing, "Without money no tangible results are possible." What did a city get in exchange for this investment? In four words, "civilization," "convenience," "health," and "beauty." To Moody, the foe of city planning in America was not active opposition but poor salesmanship. The key to success was to get the average citizen to pay serious attention to the issues and then "stir him to action when convinced." Moody believed that elected officials lacked sufficient focus to accomplish this, and so a group like the Chicago Plan Commission was required. While he expressed admiration for Burnham and Wacker as promoters, Moody understood better than they did that in a polyglot urban democracy, unlike Napoleon III's Paris, no plan could go forward simply by decree or just because the Commercial Club wanted it. The *Plan of Chicago* needed to be sold to Chicago at large by people like him, whom he characterized as salesmen not only of "civilization" but also of "harmony."

Under Moody's direction, the commission embarked on a multidimensional promotional campaign. He, Wacker, and commission staff member Eugene Taylor became a de facto three-man lecture bureau. In the seven years after Moody was hired, they were indefatigable, presenting by Moody's calculation some five hundred talks to more than 150,000 listeners. They advertised their appearances with circulars and honed their standard spiel, winnowing the several thousand lantern slides at their disposal to about two hundred images they used repeatedly.

At the same time, Moody spread the gospel of planning through a number of publications. Of these, two were most important. *Chicago's Greatest Issue: An Official Plan* appeared in May 1911. This 93-page booklet was an inexpensively produced condensation of the *Plan of Chicago*. In *Chicago's Greatest Issue*, Moody ingeniously approached the *Plan* from the viewpoint not of the planners and their wealthy associates but of ordinary citizens, whom he called the "owners of the great corporation of Chicago." He led them step-by-step toward an understanding of why the *Plan of Chicago* was vital to their interests. He distributed *Chicago's Greatest Issue* for free to property holders

Chicago's rapid growth has been one cause of street congestion.

(Chicago Plan Commission)

FIGURE 46. In order to convince Chicagoans of the importance of remaking the city, the Chicago Plan Commission pointed out several current problems. This lantern slide is a colored photograph of downtown traffic, which the caption on the slide attributes to sudden (and unplanned) expansion. "Chicago's rapid growth has been one cause of street congestion." A. G. McGregor, photographer. Historic Architecture and Landscape Image Collection, Ryerson and Burnham Archives, The Art Institute of Chicago. Reproduction © The Art Institute of Chicago.

and those who paid more than $25 a month in rent—that is, the Chicagoans whose support Moody thought most important in upcoming bond referendums.

Moody prepared other booklets, including the enticingly titled *Chicago Can Get Fifty Million Dollars for Nothing!* (1916), which claimed that the figure named was the sum of the fees the city could collect by permitting dumping on the lakeshore plus the cash value of the land created by this fill. But his most impressive publication, in both conception and execution, was his *Wacker's Manual of the Plan of Chicago*. The first version of several editions of this book appeared in 1911.

FIGURE 47. William Weil's Chicago Band forms a circle in front of Adler and Sullivan's Garrick Theater, where this 1919 rally was held. The large signboard on the truck in front of the theater lists Chicago Plan Commission chairman Charles Wacker and Mayor William Hale Thompson as speakers. The sign appeals to both Chicagoans' pride ("Now Is Your Chance Men & Women Push Chicago Forward") and honor ("Go Forward Slip Backward Which Do You Prefer"). In 1919 voters approved bond issues totaling more than $30 million. These funds were devoted to the forest preserve and the improvement of Ashland, Michigan, Western, and Ogden avenues, as well as Robey (now Damen Avenue), Twelfth (now Roosevelt Road), and South Water (now Wacker Drive) streets. Kaufmann and Fabry Co., Chicago Historical Society (ICHi-37340).

Like *Chicago's Greatest Issue, Wacker's Manual* was a shorter and more economically produced version of the *Plan of Chicago,* though it was more substantial than *Chicago's Greatest Issue.* The first edition included a very self-congratulatory chapter on the planners. Moody negotiated the inclusion of *Wacker's Manual* in the public school eighth-grade civics curriculum. The school edition eliminated the section praising the planners but added long lists of study questions (these lists were trimmed in later reprints) following each chapter, and it came with a supplementary teacher's manual. Adoption of the

Manual by the schools was no doubt facilitated by the fact that Frank Bennett was vice president of both the Chicago Plan Commission and the Board of Education. Approximately seventy thousand copies were published and distributed by 1920.

Making *Wacker's Manual* a required textbook reflected Moody's belief that "the ultimate solution of all major problems of American cities lies in the education of our children to their responsibility as the future owners of our municipalities and the arbiters of their governmental destinies." The planners picked eighth graders, Moody explained, because students at this age were old enough to understand the issues but still young enough to be impressionable. Besides, many Chicago youth ended their education at this point, so it was the last chance to appeal to a large captive audience. Moody hoped, evidently with some success, that schoolchildren versed in the *Plan* would in turn educate their parents. He invited teachers and administrators to a banquet in their honor and asked for their advice on how *Wacker's Manual* might be improved.

Moody also deployed the most up-to-date medium of the day. Under his supervision, the Chicago Plan Commission produced a two-reel promotional film, titled *A Tale of One City,* which was shown in more than sixty theaters throughout the city. The premiere screening, in Moody's words, "packed the house to capacity" with an audience that "was as representative as a grand opera occasion." But Moody focused most of all on the print media. Magazines published dozens of articles on the *Plan* and the Chicago Plan Commission, almost all of them favorable. Some were written by Chicago Plan Commission and Commercial Club members, including Charles Hutchinson, Charles Dawes, and John Shedd. Former Harvard University president Charles W. Eliot, who had appointed Burnham to a committee advising the university on its physical plan, commented in the *Century,* "We here see in action democratic enlightened collectivism coming in to repair the damage caused by exaggerated democratic individualism."

Try as they might, Wacker and Moody could not guarantee that all the responses would be positive. Well before Moody was hired, numerous individuals, including some wealthy Chicagoans, raised

FIGURE 48. The plans that Chicago made for itself attracted attention far and wide, as did its method of promoting these plans by teaching them to schoolchildren. "Chicago Children Study Big City Betterment Plan," *Brooklyn Daily Eagle*, November 17, 1912. Historic Architecture and Landscape Image Collection, Ryerson and Burnham Archives, The Art Institute of Chicago. Reproduction © The Art Institute of Chicago.

one of the most persistent criticisms of the *Plan:* for all its environmentalist slant, it pays scant attention to housing or the day-to-day lives of working people. George E. Hooker of the City Club, writing in the *Survey* shortly after the *Plan of Chicago* was released, charged that in addition to failing to address housing, the *Plan* did not deal effectively with transportation in the heart of the city. Some critiques were more pointed. John Fitzpatrick, president of the Chicago

Federation of Labor, refused Mayor Busse's invitation to serve on the Chicago Plan Commission. Fitzpatrick complained that the commission's main purpose was to assist commercial and industrial interests, who were guilty of working their employees "long hours at starvation wages." Fitzpatrick continued, "I know something about the conditions that the workers in Chicago have to contend with, and when you talk about beautifying Chicago industrially and commercially and ignore the cry of despair among the men, women, and children whose only fault is that they must toil to live, [it] makes one hesitate and ask if we are in the era before Christ or in the twentieth century of Christianity."

One of the most detailed attacks on the *Plan* came in a series of articles in the *Public,* the Chicago-based periodical that called itself the "National Journal of Fundamental Democracy" and "A Weekly Narrative of History in the Making." Long suspicious of the motives of supposedly civic-minded businessmen, the *Public* stated in the first article, "The working masses of Chicago . . . have little use for the Commercial Club or any of its recommendations." The *Public* said

FIGURE 49. Daniel and Margaret Burnham's grave site in Graceland Cemetery. As the plaque indicates, Margaret Sherman Burnham survived her husband by more than thirty years. Stefani Foster, Academic Technologies, Northwestern University.

that it would nevertheless try to evaluate the *Plan of Chicago* with an open mind. Be that as it may, in its next article on the subject, the magazine accused the planners of being anything but disinterested or munificent, since they would profit from the changes they proposed while Chicago's citizens footed the bills. The *Plan* in fact did not deal with issues that affected most people below the privileged class, the *Public* contended. In its March 7, 1913, issue, the magazine praised George Hooker's description of the Chicago Plan Commission as a group of boosters, not experts, who were all too willing to put corrupt aldermen like John Coughlin and Mike Kenna on key policy committees. It asserted that Chicago needed and deserved to have true experts do the planning. The members of the Commercial Club were, in a word, unqualified. "Probably no other large city in the world is so badly bedeviled as Chicago by grossly selfish interests masquerading as public benefactors," the *Public* claimed.

Although such criticisms emerged, the early reception of the *Plan of Chicago* was overwhelmingly flattering, which greatly pleased Daniel Burnham. While he continued to speak and write in favor of the *Plan's* implementation, Burnham entrusted the burden of promotion to Wacker, Moody, and the members of the Commercial Club and the Chicago Plan Commission. He had already given more time and effort to remaking Chicago than anyone could reasonably ask, he still had his busy architectural firm to oversee, he enjoyed his European vacations, and he had accepted other posts. President Taft had appointed Burnham the first chairman of the new U.S. Commission of Fine Arts. Its work included advising on the proposed Lincoln Memorial at the west end of the Mall, which Burnham had helped redesign a decade earlier.

By the time the *Plan of Chicago* appeared, Burnham's already uncertain health and his prodigious energy were in decline. Daniel Hudson Burnham died on June 1, 1912, in Heidelberg, Germany. Word reached Chicago just before a performance by the Chicago Symphony Orchestra at the North Shore (now Ravinia) Festival. Burnham was on the boards of both the orchestra and the festival. As a farewell salute, the orchestra added the funeral march from Wagner's *Die Götterdämmerung* to its scheduled program. Burnham was cremated and his ashes were placed in Graceland Cemetery. Sixteen years earlier he had begun his planning of Chicago with a proposal to create a new lakefront recreation area by filling in the shoreline between Grant Park and Jackson Park. Almost immediately after his death, the successful campaign began to name this large stretch of manmade lakefront land Burnham Park.

CHAPTER EIGHT

IMPLEMENTATION

Trying to determine the extent to which the city of Chicago implemented the *Plan of Chicago* is a complicated task. The *Plan* includes some recommendations that were proposed in one form or another before the Merchants Club hired Daniel Burnham, and so these proposals cannot be attributed solely to the *Plan,* whether they were followed or not. Among these recommendations are the "boulevarding" of Michigan Avenue, the creation of more parkland along the lake with fill, and the landscaping of Grant Park in a formal rather than "natural" style. In other instances, ideas suggested by the *Plan* underwent considerable modification along the way to realization. The design of Wacker Drive, for example, did not rise to the aesthetic standards that Burnham championed in his desire that the Chicago River would evoke the Seine and the city as a whole resemble Paris.

Some have also argued that the *Plan* did not make much practical difference in the evolution of Chicago's built environment. They claim that the city would have done several of the things the *Plan* proposed—such as widening many streets, building Union Station, and establishing the forest preserve—whether or not it had been published. One could add that since Chicago rejected or at least failed to implement as many of the *Plan*'s recommendations as it adopted— most notably the monumental Civic Center at Congress and Halsted— this makes it even harder to say what the *Plan*'s precise influence has been. By this logic, the *Plan of Chicago*'s fame is perhaps attributable less to the fact that it was so directly and extensively implemented than to the high profile of Burnham and the Commercial Club, the eloquence of the *Plan*'s prose style, the splendor of Guerin's and Janin's drawings, and the energy of Wacker and Moody.

This view is as much a simplification as is the assertion that the thinking behind the *Plan* was entirely original or that the *Plan* alone set the agenda of improvements in twentieth-century Chicago. To go through its chapters line by line to see where a certain idea came from and where it did or did not lead would be a fascinating though very challenging exercise in how and why Chicago developed in certain ways rather than others. It is perhaps more useful to approach the *Plan*'s originality and influence in a more general sense. While it is not always possible to ascertain whether Burnham and his fellow planners were the first to formulate this proposal or that, or how much of what actually happened is attributable to them, it is safe to assume that their support for any measure was taken very seriously. And though over the past century Chicago has followed some of these proposals only partially and often in altered form, it is interesting and worthwhile to consider the extent to which the city embodies the spirit if not always the precise letter of the *Plan*.

The implementation of the *Plan of Chicago* is inseparable from the continuing efforts to promote it. During his nine years as managing director of the Chicago Plan Commission, Walter Moody seized every chance he could find or his ingenuity could create to sell the idea of planning and the contents of this particular plan to virtually every man, woman, and child in the city. When World War I disrupted Chicago's economy, Moody issued a pamphlet declaring that a top priority was to provide employment for returning soldiers, and that the *Plan* provided a splendid way to find them jobs. "The best opportunity for this is work on Chicago's great public improvements," he wrote. Moody even raised the enactment of the *Plan* to a sacred calling. On Sunday, January 19, 1919, some eighty Chicago churches participated in what were called Nehemiah Day services. The ministers of these congregations agreed to take the words of the Old Testament prophet Nehemiah—"Therefore we, His servants, will arise and build"—as the basis of their sermons, in which they would advocate the implementation of the *Plan of Chicago*.

Moody died in 1920 at the age of forty-six. Eugene Taylor, his associate on the Chicago Plan Commission staff, succeeded him as managing director and remained in the job for the next twenty-two years. The commission continued to publish booklets with attention-getting titles, such as 1921's *An Appeal to the Businessman,* which argues that the best way to reduce local unemployment was to undertake construction projects of the kind the *Plan* proposed, a suggestion that the federal government followed during the Depression years of the 1930s. In 1924 the commission produced *An S-O-S to the Public Spirited Citizens of Chicago,* which Chairman Charles Wacker described in a speech as "a warning to the citizens not to lag in their support of the Chicago Plan." Wacker stated that Chicagoans "must push the projects in the *Plan* to a speedy completion." He also appealed to the state legislature to increase the city's ability to borrow money for such projects. Wacker's remarks came in his 1926 farewell address as chairman of the commission after seventeen years of extraordinary service. James Simpson, the head of Marshall Field's, took over for the following nine years.

The commission's aims, composition, and status changed considerably over time. Moody's death and the inevitable decline in zeal from the first group of commissioners' initial dedication led to a reduction in the commission's activities, including the disappearance of *Wacker's Manual* from the schools. Several of those who once devoted themselves single-mindedly to the *Plan*'s implementation now focused on other, albeit related, efforts. One of the most important of these was Chicago's earliest zoning regulations. Edward Bennett, now consulting architect for the Chicago Plan Commission, helped draft the 1923 zoning ordinance. Both Charles Wacker and Eugene Taylor served on the new Zoning Commission, which dealt with some of the issues that were previously on the agenda of the Chicago Plan Commission. By the 1930s the number of the commission's members had diminished, and new appointees had different priorities than the original ones. In 1939, against the advice Walter Moody had once given, the commission became part of the city government rather than an external semi-public advocacy group. Its size was reduced to twelve members, and it had little effective power.

The name "Chicago Plan Commission" has persisted through a number of administrative reorganizations, including the establishment of the Chicago Department of City Planning in 1957, which itself has undergone multiple permutations. Today the Chicago Plan Commission is part of the city of Chicago's Department of Planning and Development. It consists of nineteen people, including aldermen, other public officials, and citizens appointed by the mayor, who is also a member. Its primary duties are to approve or disapprove of initiatives by any public body or agency to acquire, dispose of, or change any property in the city, and to review certain land-use proposals, including those relating to lakefront preservation. It does not have statutory power to enforce its decisions, however.

In many respects, the three-decade era of the Chicago Plan Commission as originally constituted was a great success. Moody, Taylor, Wacker, and Simpson developed a working relationship with a series of mayors between 1909 and 1931, starting with Fred Busse and including Carter Harrison II, William Hale Thompson, William Dever, and then Thompson again. They also were able to convince voters to fund commission-supported initiatives. Between 1912 and 1931, Chicagoans approved some eighty-six *Plan*-related bond issues covering seventeen different projects with a combined cost of $234 million. Only at the end of the period did voters begin to turn down bond issues. This was due to the scandals in the administration of Thompson, who barely evaded prison but nonetheless trounced the honest and capable Dever in the 1927 election.

The first of the bond issues, and the first of many *Plan*-supported street-widening projects, involved the reconstruction of Twelfth Street (Roosevelt Road). The history of this improvement gives a sense of the complexities facing all efforts to reconstruct Chicago. On January 19, 1910, the Chicago Plan Commission recommended the improvement of Twelfth Street as the *Plan* proposed, and on April 5, 1911, the city council voted 46–10 in favor of an ordinance to widen Twelfth Street from 60 to 118 feet between Michigan Avenue and Canal Street and from 60 to 108 feet between Canal Street and Ashland Avenue, as well as to link these two sections with a new bridge across the South Branch of the Chicago River. The Harrison administration appraised the value of local real estate (of thousands of lots assessed, 302 were eventually taken, with compensation to the owners), determined which properties would be subject to special assessments, received consent from twelve different railroads whose land was affected, and obtained cooperation from the Sanitary District. (Other improvements that, unlike the Twelfth Street project, related to the harbor and the lakeshore required the permission of the United States War Department, as the Department of Defense was then called.)

The voters approved the first of two Twelfth Street bond issues in 1912, but work did not begin until four years later because of legal actions regarding compensation for seized property. On December 20, 1917, the city marked the completion of a portion of the work with a civic celebration that drew an estimated 100,000 people. From a speakers' stand erected at Twelfth and Halsted, county judge Thomas F. Scully told the crowd, with typical Chicago modesty, "We are here tonight to do honor to the greatest public improvement ever completed by this or any other municipality in the world." Continuing legal problems and difficulties in obtaining steel for civilian purposes during World War I delayed the bridge's construction. In addition, another bond referendum was required in 1919. In 1927 the commission proudly reported that the entire project was almost finished, with the notable exception of the bridge, which could not be completed until another commission recommendation, the straightening of the Chicago River, was accomplished.

Two other major street projects involved Michigan Avenue and Wacker Drive. Their improvement followed a sequence of steps similar to the Twelfth Street widening. As might have been predicted, the commission's Michigan Avenue proposal faced delays due to stiff resistance from local property owners (opponents hired more than two hundred lawyers), as well as to wartime shortages. While Michigan Avenue as actually reconstructed does not precisely resemble Guerin's renderings, the city did substantially adhere to the *Plan of Chicago*'s recommendation that the street be transformed into a much wider

FIGURE 50. This image of Michigan Avenue above Randolph Street before it was widened is from Walter Moody's book *What of the City?* (1919). The extent to which the boulevard abruptly and dramatically narrowed is clearly evident. The widening of this part of the street began on April 13, 1918, with Mayor William Hale Thompson at the head of the ceremonial wrecking crew. Northwestern University Library.

two-level boulevard that crosses the river by means of a double-decker bridge.

The widening required that the city purchase a total of fifty-one properties on the east side of Michigan Avenue south of the bridge and the west side of Pine Street (soon to be renamed Michigan Avenue once the bridge created a continuous boulevard) north of it. The bridge opened on May 14, 1920, with another gala celebration. The Wrigley Building (1921) and the Tribune Tower (1925) soon anchored the south end of the former Pine Street and what became known as the Magnificent Mile. The Chicago Plan Commission boasted that by 1925 the new bridge carried more than seven times the traffic of the old Rush Street Bridge (which was removed), and that the $16 million spent on Michigan Avenue had already paid for itself six times over in increased property values.

FIGURE 51. This dazzling photograph was probably taken in 1925. The vantage point seems to be the Tribune Tower (1925). The London Guarantee and Accident Building (1923, now 360 North Michigan Avenue) and both the Wrigley Building (1921) and its Annex (1924) are completed, while Wacker Drive, which opened in 1926, is under construction. Grant Park is still largely undeveloped. Illinois Central facilities dominate the area south of the river and east of the buildings that line the east side of a widened Michigan Avenue. Kaufmann & Fabry, Chicago Historical Society (ICHi-38229).

The commission recommended in 1917 that the city convert the crowded South Market Street wholesale area just south of the Main Branch of the Chicago River into a double-level public thoroughfare. This adhered to the *Plan*'s goal of routing commercial traffic around the Loop while also making the riverfront more attractive. The ensuing project required a heroic feat of civil engineering. Work began in 1924 and proceeded one section at a time, with crews digging twenty-four hours a day to get down to the bedrock 118 feet below, then pouring thousands of yards of structural concrete in record time. On October 20, 1926, Mayor Dever officiated at the opening of the new roadway. Upon taking office in 1923, Dever had appointed A. A. Sprague II, a member of the Commercial Club and a *Plan* advocate, commissioner of public works. Charles Wacker, after whom the new thoroughfare was named, was too ill to attend the opening.

Of other road projects suggested or inspired by the *Plan,* the extension of Ogden Avenue northeast from Randolph Street to Clark Street (later shortened to terminate, except for an isolated segment,

FIGURE 52. Although this photograph, taken from an upper floor in the Tribune Tower, dates from 1935, the area has much the same look today. Fred Korth, Chicago Historical Society (ICHi-22457).

just north of Chicago Avenue) was the only new major diagonal constructed of the several that the *Plan* had recommended. Many other existing streets were widened, however, including twenty-six miles of Western Avenue and twenty miles of Ashland Avenue. Sheridan Road was likewise enlarged to accommodate increased traffic, though it was not made into the highway to Milwaukee that the planners had called for. The major roadways encircling the city at different distances were also improved, as the *Plan* had also proposed, and a Chicago Regional Planning Association was established in 1923 with the responsibility of administering area highways. Just as the Civic Center was never built, Congress Street never became the

FIGURE 53. The Civic Center was never constructed, and its proposed location became instead one of the world's busiest highway intersections, the Circle Interchange, pictured here in 1973. The Kennedy Expressway runs north of the interchange and can be seen at the top of the photograph. The Ryan Expressway reaches south, the Eisenhower to the west, and Congress Parkway runs east from the Circle into the area of downtown just south of the Loop. The University of Illinois's Chicago campus, once known as Circle Campus for its proximity to the interchange, can be seen in the lower left corner of the photo. Halsted Street extends north and south just west of the interchange. Chicago Historical Society (ICHi-37483).

major east-west "Axis of Chicago" that Burnham and his fellow planners had eagerly desired.

The straightening of the South Branch of the Chicago River was another astonishing piece of engineering. The South Branch has always run approximately due south from the Main Branch for a few blocks, but up to the late 1920s it then edged east a bit, cutting off Franklin Street at about Van Buren Street. Starting at Polk Street, it began an even more marked eastward bend of about three blocks. By the time it reached Fifteenth Street, it was only about 150 feet west of Clark Street. As a result, it blocked the southward extension of Franklin, Wells, Sherman, and LaSalle streets. Complicating the situation was that railroad tracks occupied almost all of the land bordered by the South Branch and Polk, State, and Sixteenth streets.

With the railroads pushing for the construction of a new Union Station that would serve multiple passenger lines (also proposed by the *Plan of Chicago*), the Chicago Plan Commission helped persuade the city council to include in the ordinance approving the station a provision for straightening the South Branch, along with several other street-improvement and bridge-construction recommendations from the *Plan*. After considerably more negotiations, studies by the new Chicago Railway Terminal Commission, and agreements about the railroad property transfers that would be necessary if the city changed the river's course, the city council passed an ordinance on July 8, 1926, to straighten the river between Polk and Eighteenth streets. Voters backed the related bond issue in the election of April 5, 1927, and by 1930 the city had completed the project. The north-south streets west of Clark Street and east of the Chicago River were not extended southward significantly, however.

The reorganization of some of the haphazard layout of tracks and the construction of Union Station (1925) were arguably the closest the city came to enacting specific rail recommendations from the *Plan of Chicago*. The Chicago Plan Commission wanted the station to be constructed at Roosevelt and Canal in order to relieve congestion in the downtown, but it was ultimately built at Jackson and Canal. The older downtown stations that the planners hoped to close through

FIGURE 54. This photograph was taken in 1929, a year before the river-straightening project was completed. The view is from the south, toward downtown, and both the river's old path and its new one are visible. The photograph also makes evident how much of the real estate in this area was devoted to railroad tracks and yards. Chicago Aerial Survey Company, Chicago Historical Society (ICHi-05776).

consolidation remained in use for decades. The commission never persuaded the railroads to back the construction of the enormous station the *Plan* recommended for the south side of Twelfth Street. The Pennsylvania Railroad did agree not to build its new freight terminal at Halsted and Congress, the site of the proposed Civic Center, but the terminal's construction at 323 West Polk Street did not open up the downtown as much as the commission had hoped. The diminishment of rail congestion in the center of the city as the twentieth century progressed was attributable mainly to the decline of long-distance travel and shipping by train. Chicago delayed building a much-needed subway system for several decades, and when construction of the State Street line finally began in 1938 (the first trains started running in 1943), the project was more modest than the proposals made by the *Plan* and in several other reports since 1909.

The *Plan of Chicago* called for transforming the city's lakefront, by means of filling and landscaping, into one continuous and spectacular public park that would enable more people to enjoy the city's most wondrous natural feature. The filling of the lakeshore south of Fourteenth Street began in 1917 and reached Jackson Park thirteen years later, but the long lagoon Burnham had first designed in the 1890s was not built. The city did construct beaches and other amenities, however, as well as Soldier Field (1924), located just south of the new Field Museum. East of Soldier Field and the Field Museum, it created Northerly Island, which follows the *Plan* quite closely. The filled land that constitutes the access to Northerly Island and the island itself became the site of the Shedd Aquarium (1929), the Adler Planetarium (1930), the Century of Progress International Exposition of 1933–34, and, shortly after World War II, the Meigs Field Airport.

Lincoln Park, meanwhile, expanded farther northward and outward, reaching Diversey Parkway by the early 1920s, Montrose Avenue by the end of the decade, and Foster Avenue by 1933 (it did not extend to its current northern terminus at Hollywood Avenue until the 1950s). In 1916 the city completed Municipal (soon Navy) Pier, one of the two man-made extensions into the lake recommended by the *Plan,* though the city built the pier at Grand Avenue and not, as the *Plan* had recommended, at Chicago Avenue. The pier's southern counterpart, at Twenty-second Street, was never constructed.

The *Plan* intended Grant Park—with its northern and southern boundaries at Randolph and Twelfth streets—to be the cultural center of the city. The crown jewel would be the Field Museum, centered on the Congress Street "Axis of Chicago," with the Crerar Library nearby. When the lawsuits filed by Montgomery Ward prevented this, the location of the Field Museum was moved to just south of Grant Park, and the Crerar Library constructed its building on the northwest corner of Michigan Avenue and Randolph Street, opposite both the Chicago Public Library and Grant Park (it subsequently moved twice more, first to the campus of the Illinois Institute of Technology

FIGURE 55. Municipal Pier was built between 1913 and 1916 (this photograph was taken in 1914). Only the northern of the two proposed piers was built, and it was located at Grand Avenue instead of Chicago Avenue. Municipal Pier was named Navy Pier in the 1920s. Three thousand feet long and almost three hundred feet wide, it contained harbor facilities, warehouse sheds, railroad tracks, office space, and, at the eastern end, the ballroom that is still there. *Chicago Daily News,* Chicago Historical Society (DN-0063456).

in 1962 and then to its current location at the University of Chicago in 1984). The city turned its efforts to landscaping the park and depressing the Illinois Central tracks by building up the land around them. Both measures were very much in the spirit of the *Plan.*

Burnham's first design for Grant Park placed a fountain east of the Field Museum in the approximate spot of Buckingham Fountain, which was completed in 1927 and became one of Chicago's signature landmarks. Burnham's fellow planners, who included several trustees of the Art Institute, advocated an expansion of that museum's facilities to include more gallery space, studios, a school, and administrative offices, as well as open-air loggias and gardens. When the Montgomery Ward cases blocked building anything above grade in the park, the Art Institute dealt with this restriction by erecting a new wing over the Illinois Central tracks just behind the original building. The Art Institute adopted equally ingenious measures when it constructed the George Alexander McKinlock Jr. Memorial Court and the Kenneth Sawyer Goodman Theatre in the mid-1920s by embedding them in filled land east of the tracks. The Goodman inaugurated its current North Loop theater building on October 20, 2000, exactly seventy-five years after the original space in the Art Institute was dedicated, with the performance of works by Chicago playwright Kenneth Sawyer Goodman, whose parents originally funded it in his memory.

The *Plan of Chicago* recommended the construction of a parkway along the lakeshore devoted to recreation and pleasure and connected to the city proper with viaducts. Work on a South Side parkway began in 1917 and reached Fifty-seventh Street by 1932, with viaducts at Twenty-third, Thirty-first, Thirty-ninth, and Forty-seventh streets.

FIGURE 56. Navy Pier, ca. 1920–21. This view of the pier is from the northeast. The ballroom was restored in 1976, but the shipping facilities behind it, which were devoted to a multitude of uses over the years and had badly deteriorated, were replaced by the current recreational and entertainment complex in 1994. Chicago Historical Society (ICHi-14115).

FIGURE 57. Grant Park in 1929, looking northwest toward Michigan Avenue. While the park lacks much of today's landscaping and structures, the basic layout is in place, Buckingham Fountain (1927) has been built, and the Art Institute has expanded over the Illinois Central tracks, which are still a very significant presence. Chicago Historical Society (ICHi-03394).

The state of Illinois paid for the parkway construction on the North Side during the Depression. This parkway stretched to Foster Avenue by 1933. The North Side extension featured a series of cloverleaf intersections providing entries and exits. Under Wacker and Moody, the Chicago Plan Commission had discussed with the South Park commissioners and the Lincoln Park Board the possibility of building a link across the Chicago River near the lakefront in order to connect Grant Park to Municipal Pier and to reduce traffic over the Michigan Avenue Bridge. The connection of the north and south portions by means of the two-level Link Bridge, with extensions north to Ohio Street and south to Monroe Street, was constructed with federal Public Works Administration funding, and it opened in 1939. The sharp turns in this roadway were not reduced until the completion of the current S-curve in 1986. The volume of traffic necessitated the construction of a new wide section between Ohio Street and Belmont Avenue.

The *Plan* urged the building of more parks and playgrounds in the city and the setting aside of natural areas in Chicago and nearby for recreation. This was in keeping with policies formulated by the Special Park Commission and the Outer Belt Commission in the first years of the twentieth century. The development of the lakeshore was the *Plan*'s most dramatic influence on park development, but the

FIGURE 58. The date of this photograph is probably the mid-1880s, shortly after construction of the home of Bertha and Potter Palmer (1882, at 1350 North Lakeshore Drive), visible on the left. At this point, Lake Shore Drive (often called the Inner Drive, to distinguish it from the limited access automobile highway later constructed on filled land to the east) was a relatively quiet boulevard used for carriage rides along the lakefront. Chicago Historical Society (ICHi-37286).

FIGURE 59. This 1955 photograph of Lake Shore Drive shows the
extension of the highway to its current terminus at Hollywood Avenue.
Calvin C. Oleson, Chicago Historical Society (ICHi-37277).

impetus the *Plan* gave to the forest preserve was much larger in scope.
The Forest Preserve District of Cook County was approved by the
voters in 1914 and established the following year, with Charles Wacker
on its board. In 1916 it acquired its first new land, located in northwest Cook County in the area now known as the Deer Grove Forest

Preserve District. The district soon added portions of the Skokie Valley. In 1921 it received a gift of eighty-three acres from Edith Rockefeller McCormick, the daughter of John D. Rockefeller, primary benefactor of the University of Chicago, and the wife of Harold McCormick, who had served on the Commercial Club's Committee on Lake Parks. This donation, to which was added over a hundred more acres purchased by the district, became the site of the Brookfield Zoo. By 1925 the Chicago Plan Commission proudly reported that the Forest Preserve District had acquired another thirty thousand acres in a broad belt "from the shore of the lake at the Indiana state line on the south to the edge of the lake again near Glencoe at the north."

In the best Progressive tradition, the Chicago Plan Commission bemoaned the inefficiency of the organization of government agencies. In 1920 it estimated that the scattering of municipal offices throughout the city cost taxpayers an extra $75,000 a year, and that the new (and still-current) City Hall had been too small even at the time it was dedicated in 1911. But the *Plan*'s most original suggestion, a unified civic center set on a vast plaza, never generated the enthusiastic support required to make it possible. Another project that occupied much of the commission's attention did come to fruition, however: a central United States Post Office on the Near West Side that could handle the astonishing volume of mail entering and leaving Chicago. The Chicago Plan Commission noted that just the *increase* in mail since the existing main post office was erected in 1906 was greater than the *combined* 1919 volume of Boston, Detroit, Cincinnati, Kansas City, and Jersey City.

The commission complained that mail service was getting progressively slower, and that it would "break down absolutely in two years if prompt relief is not had." It recommended a two-block site on Canal Street between Madison and Adams as being ideally accessible to all parts of the city and to nearby railroad stations. In June 1919 the postmaster general appointed a committee to examine the situation, with the omnipresent Charles Wacker as its chair. By 1927 the government acquired an enormous site, on Canal Street between Polk and Harrison, just to the south of where the commission recommended. The structure, the largest post office in the world at that time, opened in 1932. It was succeeded as the city's main mail-handling center in 1996 by the much smaller and more automated General Mail Facility across the street.

Daniel Burnham had died twenty years before the post office was completed, but he indirectly touched this and other buildings that were related to the implementation of the *Plan of Chicago*. The post office as well as the Field Museum, Union Station, and the Shedd Aquarium were all designed by successor firms to D. H. Burnham and Company. On some other projects, the hand of Edward H. Bennett was directly present. Bennett was only thirty-five the year the *Plan* was published. He served as consulting architect for the Chicago Plan Commission until 1930, with the Commercial Club paying his salary for the first half of this period. Bennett stayed with Burnham's firm for a few years, but he soon developed his own independent career as a city planner. His clients included Brooklyn, Cedar Rapids, Detroit, Minneapolis, Ottawa, Portland, St. Paul, and San Francisco. The Minneapolis plan, published in 1917, bears a striking resemblance to the *Plan of Chicago*.

Closer to Chicago, Bennett prepared plans for Elgin, Joliet, Winnetka, and his hometown of Lake Forest, and he later designed a civic center for Denver and various projects for other municipalities. At the request of his *Plan of Chicago* associate Charles Norton, Bennett also participated in the creation of a regional plan for New York City. He established the firm of Bennett, Parsons, and Frost, whose commissions included Buckingham Fountain. One of his designs was of a colonnade and fountain that stood near the southeast corner of Randolph Street and Michigan Avenue from 1917 to the mid-1950s. In a tribute to Bennett, Millennium Park includes a replica of this colonnade on the same site. Bennett spoke and wrote on behalf of the planning idea, and he consulted on work done by the city in implementing the proposals of the Chicago Plan Commission, including the Michigan Avenue Bridge, for which he prepared the first plans in 1910. Bennett's work for the commission encompassed dozens of projects, with all their accompanying discussions, hearings, and disputes.

In 1930 the Chicago Plan Commission abolished the position of consulting architect. It is possible that this decision reflected the need to economize at the onset of the Depression. More likely, however, it signaled that the new leadership of the commission had different views from those of its predecessors—and of Bennett. In 1929, under the auspices of the commission, Bennett had published a 44-page illustrated booklet titled *The Axis of Chicago* that one last time presented the *Plan of Chicago*'s case for making Congress Street the city's major east-west thoroughfare by widening it and extending it out to the Des Plaines River. He was soon deeply upset by the commission's proposal to abandon the Congress Street axis idea, including the Civic

FIGURE 60. This colonnade and fountain, the most traditional piece of new architecture in Millennium Park, are located near the southeast corner of Michigan Avenue and Randolph Street. A plaque on the colonnade notes that this is a replica of the original colonnade, designed by Edward Bennett, which was also situated here. Harlan Wallach, Academic Technologies, Northwestern University.

Center, and to focus on a proposal to elevate Monroe Street. Bennett protested against this in print, and he also criticized the location of the post office. But the battle was lost, and his association with the Chicago Plan Commission was over.

Bennett continued to get important work, including several buildings at Chicago's 1933–34 world's fair. He became chairman of the board of architects directing the design of the buildings in Washington's Federal Triangle, located north of the eastern section of the Mall. His firm of Bennett, Parsons, and Frost designed the Apex Building, completed in 1938 at the western tip of the Triangle. This was the last major work by Bennett, who died in 1954. His planning career thus concluded where Daniel Burnham's had begun, at the site of his senior associate's contributions to the Senate Park Commission at the turn of the century.

CHAPTER NINE

HERITAGE

With the redefinition and reconfiguration of the original Chicago Plan Commission in 1939, there was no longer any organization, committee, or agency whose central purpose was to implement the recommendations of the *Plan of Chicago*. This was not an indication that the age of urban planning in Chicago and elsewhere had reached its end, but that it was well into another phase, one that shows how pervasive the influence of the *Plan of Chicago* was. By this time, cities in this country and abroad had taken it for granted that one of the standard responsibilities of urban government was to assess the state of the built environment and establish special agencies and commissions to make recommendations about changes. The creation of the *Plan* was hardly the only source of this development, but it was probably the single most important one.

Within a few years after the publication of the *Plan of Chicago,* planning had become an established profession of its own, and planners in the United States were part of an international community of specialists who shared and debated ideas at conferences and in print about the proper structure of cities. The American Institute of Planners was established in 1917, and it later merged with the American Society of Planning Officials, which was founded in 1934, to form the American Planning Association. The American Institute of Certified Planners is the APA's professional attesting organization. Whether planners after Burnham looked to his work with admiration or disapproval, they universally acknowledged his crucial role in establishing their calling and advancing its status.

In terms of Chicago in particular, it is interesting to speculate whether particular or larger developments in the years after the dissolution of the original Chicago Plan Commission owe their origins in some way to the *Plan,* though definitive attributions of this kind remain elusive. Some might argue, for instance, that the Congress Expressway (which opened in 1956 and was renamed the Eisenhower Expressway in 1964) is an updated version of the *Plan* proposal to widen and extend Congress Street, while others might call it a desecration of the *Plan*'s idea of transforming Congress into a stately civic boulevard that would be the "Axis of Chicago." One might similarly ask if Daniel Burnham would have welcomed some projects that the *Plan of Chicago* did not specifically propose, such as Soldier Field (1924; remodeled, 2003), the Shedd Aquarium (1929, the gift of *Plan of Chicago*

FIGURE 61. Work on the Congress Parkway and Expressway (now the Eisenhower Expressway) began in 1949. The view here is west from the mammoth United States Post Office in 1951. Congress Parkway would lead into the expressway, passing through the bottom of the post office. Mildred Mead, Chicago Historical Society (ICHi-27308).

FIGURE 62. This aerial photograph of the lakefront, looking southeast, offers a view of the Field Museum (*center*), the Shedd Aquarium (*center left*), the Adler Planetarium (*top left* at the end of the parkway), Northerly Island (*top right*), and Soldier Field (*right*). Meigs Field Airport had not yet been developed on Northerly Island. At this point, Lake Shore Drive's northbound traffic was routed east of Soldier Field and the Field Museum, while the southbound lanes were located to the west. By the end of 1996, the entire highway had been moved west of the stadium and the museum, and the improvement of Roosevelt Road made possible a much more unified "museum campus" with pedestrian access to Grant Park. Howard A. Wolf, 1947, Chicago Historical Society (ICHi-00940).

Committee on Railway Terminals member John G. Shedd), or the Adler Planetarium (1930). While Burnham passionately declared that the lake was the city's one great natural feature and that the lakefront must remain open to the public, he also favored locating cultural institutions in Grant Park, and he undoubtedly would have liked the siting of the aquarium and the planetarium, and probably even the stadium.

Whether Burnham would have approved of the vast commercial trade show and convention center that is McCormick Place (1960, 1971, 1986, 1996) or the private yacht clubs currently along the lake is a tougher question to answer. It is possible to contend, based on some of his statements about the importance of protecting the lakefront as a public resource, that he would have raised strong objections to them. But he himself proposed putting an exposition building and yacht clubs in Grant Park, as well as restaurants and hotels along the lagoon he wished to construct between downtown and Jackson Park. It is very likely that Burnham, who played the central role in the staging of the World's Columbian Exposition of 1893, would have given his blessing to situating the Century of Progress International Exposition on Northerly Island and around Burnham Harbor in 1933–34. He probably also would have favored turning Municipal Pier into the lakefront public recreation, exhibition, and amusement area that Navy Pier is today. An avid traveler and a believer in serving the convenience of wealthy businessmen, he might well have been pleased by the opening of the Meigs Field Airport on Northerly Island, and he certainly would have backed the building of Midway and O'Hare airports. As a champion of the City Beautiful, he would have supported the considerable attention Chicago has devoted in recent years to improving its appearance by planting flowers and trees and by installing neighborhood decorative markers. And while he might not have selected the postmodern architectural style of some of Millennium Park's installations, Burnham would probably have appreciated how successfully the park draws local residents and tourists to the downtown lakefront.

Any discussion of the heritage of the *Plan of Chicago* and Daniel Burnham is further complicated by the iconic status both the *Plan* and Burnham have attained over the years. The *Plan* long ago ceased to be a collection of proposals and Burnham a mere architect and urban planner. They have become landmarks in the cityscape, as palpable a presence for any planner or civic leader as Michigan Avenue or Grant Park. Developers, public officials, politicians, journalists, and commentators often cite the *Plan* and Burnham not as part of a close analysis of the former's recommendations or of the latter's career in themselves, but in order to make their own point about Chicago or the proper direction of modern city life. Boosters of any number of different projects have invoked the famous exhortation "Make no little plans; they have no magic to stir men's blood," attributed to Burnham by Charles Moore, as if to suggest that to reject what they

FIGURE 63. The vantage in this bird's-eye view of the Century of Progress International Exposition, photographed ca. 1933, is looking north. While the *Plan*'s proposal for a continuous lagoon along the South Side lakefront had been abandoned, Northerly Island, on the right, forms a small lagoon to its west. At the north end of the fair, one can see Soldier Field, the Field Museum, the Shedd Aquarium, and (largely obscured by a Century of Progress tower) the Adler Planetarium. Chicago Historical Society (ICHi-31117).

are proposing is an abandonment of the defining essence of Chicago's character. Others, meanwhile, blame the "big is beautiful" view that these words convey for making the city, in their opinion at least, inimical to small-scale human needs.

Twentieth-century historian and cultural critic Lewis Mumford is among those who attacked the *Plan* for this reason. In the tradition of Louis Sullivan, who characterized Burnham as "a colossal merchandiser," Mumford criticized Burnham for being primarily interested in pumping up land values, a charge that has also been leveled at the Commercial Club, whose financial and emotional investments in Chicago mutually reinforced one another. In *The City in History:*

FIGURE 64. On March 23, 1963, Mayor Richard J. Daley hosted President John F. Kennedy at the dedication of the new passenger terminal at Chicago O'Hare International Airport. In an age of diminishing railroad traffic and increasing travel and shipping by air and road, the city's new airport and its location at the intersection of several interstate highways were essential to the city's status as a vital nexus. Chicago Historical Society (ICHi-32484).

Its Origins, Its Transformations, and Its Prospects (1961), Mumford calls the *Plan* the fullest example of twentieth-century "baroque planning," a set of ideas with "no concern for the neighborhood as an integral unit, no regard for family housing, no sufficient conception of the ordering of business and industry themselves as a necessary part of any larger achievement of urban order."

Urbanist Jane Jacobs, who has sharply disagreed with Mumford on some aspects of city planning, agrees with his condemnation of Burnham. In the introduction to her best known work, *The Death and Life of Great American Cities* (1961), Jacobs is particularly disparaging of Burnham's emphasis on civic centers and monumental designs, which, she contends, have degraded rather than improved the neighborhoods around them. It is true that neither the text nor the illustrations of the *Plan* pay much attention to the quality of urban street life on which Jacobs focuses so much concern, or to how the individual actually experiences the city, other than as a grid to move across as efficiently as possible. With few exceptions, people are either entirely missing from Guerin's and Janin's drawings or completely overwhelmed by the massive scale of the buildings.

Mumford observes, however, that despite the "ruthless overriding of historical realities" implicit in Burnham's famous quotation about making no little plans, "there was a measure of deep human insight" in it as well. Burnham's planning vision, whether sound or misguided, does in fact stir the blood because it so powerfully expresses the desire to be able to reach beyond piecemeal solutions and act efficaciously on the grandest scale. At the very moment when life became modern and Americans realized that twentieth-century urban experience was fraught with limitations and contingencies, Burnham insisted that if we are just bold and brave and determined enough, it is possible to master time and space and make all things right. The *Plan*'s very real historical appeal lies precisely in the fact that it proclaims history is no match for human will and cities can determine rather than merely accept their fate.

As urban historian Carl Abbott points out, the *Plan of Chicago* is the defining document of an era that extends from the 1880s to the 1920s, when "public and private interests coalesced around efforts to integrate the sprawling metropolis." Abbott groups the *Plan* with the work of the city's park boards, the Sanitary District, and the early years of the Chicago Plan Commission. Viewed in this context, the *Plan*'s most important heritage is the persistence of the idea that it is necessary to think not only big but also comprehensively. Chicago, the *Plan* contends, is part of a region that consists of many components, an interdependent system in which any problem or improvement reverberates through the metropolitan area as a whole. Abbott observes that since the 1930s the goals of planning "have become more specialized or limited," reflecting the "gradual erosion and fragmentation"

FIGURE 65. Guerin's view of upper Michigan Avenue as a continuous boulevard. Even on this street whose main purpose was personal enjoyment and pleasure, the titanic scale makes the individuals out for a ride, a stroll, or some shopping appear tiny and scattered. In several *Plan* drawings of the downtown, people are even smaller or the streets are completely deserted. Chicago Historical Society (ICHi-39070_6t).

of the "civic vision" of the previous era. This is not necessarily an unfortunate development, for it is possible—Burnham's supposed scorn for "little" plans notwithstanding—that more specialized or limited proposals may have a better chance of successful realization than bigger ones, and they may end up serving a greater number and variety of people more effectively.

Abbott's description of the narrowing focus of plans is accurate. Public or semi-public agencies and neighborhood or private groups have prepared dozens of planning studies and documents that deal with defined parts of the built environment of Chicago or that aim to improve a specific aspect of city life. As early as 1913, the City Club of Chicago sponsored a competition to encourage better planning of the outskirts of the city, with the goal of creating attractive and functional residential areas. During the late 1930s and early 1940s, proposals focused separately on parks and parkways, a new subway system, and water and sewerage facilities. In the following decade, planners concentrated on reviving the city's industrial base and making older areas of Chicago more appealing places to live. This was a response to the aging of the city's infrastructure, factories, and housing stock, in part because of deferred maintenance due to the Depression and then the war.

In 1909 the planners were concerned with how to continue attracting people to Chicago. Following World War II, the issue was how to get them to stay. After peaking in the early 1950s, Chicago's population began to decline. Meanwhile, the percentage of African Americans rapidly rose from 8.2 percent in 1940 to 13.6 percent a decade later. As a result, a not very hidden question in some proposals was how to maintain a sense of community in a city sharply divided by race, which, many argued, was an important factor in the migration of white Chicagoans to the suburbs. It was hardly the only factor behind this movement, which drew the attention of planners. In July 1943, before the full boom of towns surrounding the city, the Chicago Plan Commission issued a report titled *Building New Neighborhoods,* stating that its purpose was to make suburban-style residences in the city that would keep Chicagoans in Chicago.

FIGURE 66. This Guerin drawing of a proposed plaza west of the Field Museum in Grant Park, which resembles an impressionist urban scene, is one of the few that depicts a lively street life. Chicago Historical Society (ICHi-39070_70).

The previous year the commission had published *Forty-four Cities in the City of Chicago,* which highlighted what made individual neighborhoods in the city so special. In 1946 it collaborated with the Woodlawn Planning Committee to use that South Side neighborhood as an example of how to analyze the problems facing "middle-aged" Chicago residential areas. The purpose of this study was to find a way to revitalize communities through better use of land, reconstruction of physical facilities, and improved services. In 1951 the commission released a report on industry proposing zoning changes and other measures to redevelop blighted homes and factories and to cluster the latter

more efficiently. Five years later a group at the University of Chicago working for the city's Community Conservation Board analyzed how the Hyde Park–Kenwood neighborhood might be made more orderly and stable by clearing slums, constructing better housing, and considering what other steps might contribute to a viable community.

The Burnham "make no little plans" credo revived considerably under Mayor Richard J. Daley, who won the first of six consecutive elections in the spring of 1955. At the end of the 1940s, the Chicago Plan Commission had proposed a modern civic center complex between Madison and Van Buren streets just east of the river, but nothing came of this. Three years into Daley's first term, Chicago's new Department of City Planning prepared the *Development Plan for the*

Central Area of Chicago. Among its recommendations that have been extensively enacted under Daley's and succeeding administrations are the Civic Center (1965, now the Richard J. Daley Center) east of the City Hall–County Building (1911), the nearby State of Illinois Center (1985, now the James R. Thompson Center) and multi-structure Federal Center (1964, 1974, 1991), the S-curve along Lake Shore Drive by the Link Bridge (1986), the relocation of the University of Illinois at Chicago from Navy Pier to its current Near West Side campus (1965), residential development south of the Loop and on the Near North Side, and the major construction south of the Main Branch of the Chicago River and east of Michigan Avenue.

As its name indicates, the *Development Plan for the Central Area,* ambitious as it was, covered only the part of the city discussed in the *Plan of Chicago*'s chapter "The Heart of Chicago." The 1972 *Lakefront Plan of Chicago* likewise focused just on the area specified in its title, while the *Chicago 21* plan of 1973 was an updating of the *Development Plan for the Central Area.* The *Lakefront Plan* aimed at consolidating public control of the lakefront, maintaining and enhancing the lakeshore parks and water quality, and assuring that Lake Shore Drive retained the qualities of a scenic parkway. *Chicago 21* confronted what it saw as the continuing deterioration of the central city, especially for purposes other than work. While its State Street Mall proposal was a notable failure as an attempt to compete with outlying shopping centers, the construction of the Harold Washington Library Center (1991), improvements in transportation, the location of some city colleges and private university facilities in or near the Loop, and the recent residential boom throughout the central area demonstrate the considerable influence of *Chicago 21* proposals.

The latest iteration of a city-sponsored plan for the downtown is the *Central Area Plan* of 2003, which was prepared by the departments of Planning and Development, Transportation, and Environment of the administration of Mayor Richard M. Daley. Predicting that by 2020 there will be more jobs, residents, tourists, students, and retail establishments in the Central Area, this document calls for some of the same things the *Plan of Chicago* discussed a century ago, notably better public transportation facilities and further development of the

FIGURE 67. The construction of the Harold Washington Library Center (1991) at 400 South State Street was intended both to replace a century-old facility (now the Chicago Cultural Center, on Michigan Avenue, between Randolph and Washington streets) and to revitalize the South Loop. John McCarthy, Chicago Historical Society (ICHi-38003).

waterfront for public use. But it speaks more to current concerns than those of 1909 when it discusses the need for Chicago to be a sustainable city that respects and preserves its past.

Even if none of these plans are as all-encompassing as the *Plan of Chicago,* several of them claimed to be part of its heritage. In his foreword to the *Chicago 21* plan, Mayor Richard J. Daley notes the inspiration of "Burnham's dream" that "gave great emphasis to the central area." The 1949 proposal for a civic center contended that it was in the spirit of the *Plan* even if it rejected the *Plan*'s neoclassical aesthetics. It argued for new government buildings that would be state-of-the-art high-rises (as the Daley Center turned out to be) quite different from the *Plan*'s domed colossus. *Chicago 21* asserts that "the present generation, while enjoying the fruits of the Burnham Plan, can also contribute to the heritage of future generations" with a "soundly conceived" civic center that is "conveniently located" and "appropriately designed."

Plans continued to appear that were as broad in scope as the *Plan of Chicago,* though they differed from the *Plan* at least as much as they resembled it. The Chicago Plan Commission's 1966 *Comprehensive Plan of Chicago* discussed the city as a whole, but it emphasized a quality-of-life agenda much more than Burnham and the Commercial Club had done. It examined the need to improve living conditions for families, working people, and the disadvantaged. Issued shortly before the urban riots of the late 1960s and at a time when Chicago's era as an industrial giant was nearing its end, the *Comprehensive Plan* was concerned with countering residential segregation and creating more service-economy jobs, as well as improving housing, transportation, recreational facilities, and public education. As Carl Abbott points out, however, devising effective ways to improve society has been a harder task for planners than implementing physical changes. Finding good housing for poor and middle-class residents, countering racial segregation, and maintaining a high-quality school system that successfully serves all of its students have proved to be elusive goals.

Two proposals stand out as direct heirs to the *Plan of Chicago,* and both have sound claims to the pedigree. One of the coauthors of the Chicago Regional Planning Association's 1956 *Planning the Region of Chicago* was none other than architect Daniel H. Burnham Jr., who for thirty years had been president of the association. Burnham's coauthor was Robert Kingery (after whom the Kingery Expressway is named), the association's general manager and former director of the Illinois Department of Public Works. *Planning the Region of Chicago* is dedicated to the Merchants Club of Chicago, whose members, the lengthy dedication informs us, "have maintained their interest and have continued to direct the carrying out of the *Plan of Chicago* and, more recently, of Regional Planning in the Region of Chicago." The dedication continues, "In the twilight of their lives, the few and far-scattered survivors of the Merchants Club arranged for publication of this book." They did so "not merely as a record of outstanding accomplishments," but also "as a challenge to the young men of today to grasp and cherish the torch their forefathers kindled."

Planning the Region of Chicago, while not as luxuriously presented as the *Plan of Chicago,* otherwise closely resembles it in size, layout, and topics covered, though, as its title implies, it discusses Chicago in relation to its region more than does the *Plan.*

A more recent proposal that explicitly recalls the *Plan of Chicago* is *Chicago Metropolis 2020,* subtitled *The Chicago Plan for the Twenty-first Century,* which was published in 2001. Like the *Plan of Chicago, Chicago Metropolis 2020* was sponsored by the Commercial Club, along with the American Academy of Arts and Sciences. Its informative maps and charts and its striking photography also recall the *Plan,* as does its cover, which is an updated Jules Guerin's bird's-eye-view rendering of downtown Chicago as seen from the lake. The book's author is Chicago attorney Elmer W. Johnson, former president of the Aspen Institute and member of both sponsoring organizations. *Chicago Metropolis 2020* takes as its starting point some of the premises of the *Plan of Chicago,* most notably that Chicago is a commercial city that must plan ahead very carefully and find sensible solutions if it is to thrive. Like the *Plan* and *Planning the Region of Chicago, Chicago Metropolis 2020* talks about the necessity of thinking regionally, pointing out that the region of Chicago now includes Cook and all of the five contiguous counties.

Chicago Metropolis 2020 discusses many of the same kinds of topics as the *Plan of Chicago* and *Planning the Region of Chicago,* notably economic vitality, transportation, recreation, and land use. Harking back to the Progressive program of a century earlier, it also recommends streamlining governing agencies. Like the *Plan,* it discusses the legislation required to bring about change and the need to educate the public on the virtues of planning. But its approach is quite different from the *Plan* in some important ways. Basing its analysis on recent historical and social science scholarship, *Chicago Metropolis 2020* puts much more emphasis on the issues of better schools, expanded health and child care, and improved services for low-income families.

Since producing its book, the Chicago Metropolis 2020 organization has evolved into a group that recalls the Chicago Plan Commission. Like the commission, it sends its leaders and staff to speak with public officials and civic organizations, and it continues to publish promotional literature. But its spokespersons use PowerPoint rather

FIGURE 68. This image appears on the cover of *The Metropolis Plan: Choices for the Chicago Region*, a booklet summarizing the major goals and proposals discussed in much greater detail in *Chicago Metropolis 2020: The Chicago Plan for the Twenty-first Century*. While this view does not have a precise equivalent in the *Plan of Chicago*, it evokes the *Plan*'s bird's-eye views of the city. A significant difference is that the vantage here is from a greater distance than most of the Guerin drawings, reflecting *Chicago Metropolis 2020*'s emphasis on the broad region that includes Chicago and not just on the city itself. Mitchell A. Markovitz, Chicago Metropolis 2020.

than lantern slides to make their presentations, and some of its publications either appear on the Web or come with a CD-ROM. Following the example of *Wacker's Manual,* Chicago Metropolis 2020 aims to capture the interest of younger people, though its means is not a civics textbook with review questions but a Web-based computer game that features a street-smart character named Metro Joe.

In some ways, then, planning for the future of Chicago has come full circle in the century that has passed since the publication of the *Plan of Chicago,* but in other ways it has changed considerably. *Chicago Metropolis 2020* is based on the idea that public and private interests can and must league together to remake a metropolitan community for the benefit of everyone. It believes, as did the *Plan,* that idealistic and practical goals are not at odds with each other. It is similarly concerned with sustaining Chicago's growth by disciplining it. And the "make no little plans" philosophy informs both documents. But there is a fuller recognition now that the planning effort requires facing more complex human issues than can be solved by building more parks, enforcing sanitary measures, and other mainly design and engineering solutions that do not take fully into account the social as well as physical structure of the metropolis.

The idea of comprehensive community planning faces stiff resistance from the cherished idea that people should be able to do with their lives and their property as they wish. There are many more politically empowered interest groups now than there were in 1909 who want their needs to be met and their desires to be fulfilled. This is a good thing for a truly democratic society, but it makes it hard to find or build a consensus in support of a comprehensive regional plan for a place as large and diverse as metropolitan Chicago. What keeps the planning idea alive and well in Chicago and other cities is a continuing faith in both city life and in the belief that it should, can, and must constantly be remade for the better.

BIBLIOGRAPHICAL ESSAY

Any understanding of the *Plan of Chicago* must begin with the *Plan* itself as it originally appeared. While only 1,650 copies of the *Plan* were printed, there have been two excellent facsimile editions in which the illustrations as well as the text are carefully reproduced. The first was published by Da Capo Press (New York, 1970), the second by Princeton Architectural Press (New York, 1993). The complete volume, including all the illustrations, is also available online in the electronic edition of the *Encyclopedia of Chicago,* at http:// www.encyclopedia.chicagohistory.org/pages/10417.html. The home page of this edition of the *Encyclopedia of Chicago* is http://www .encyclopedia.chicagohistory.org. The *Plan* can also be accessed through the electronic edition's "Interpretive Digital Essay: The *Plan of Chicago,*" which begins at http://www.encyclopedia.chicagohistory .org/pages/10537.html.

In addition, the electronic edition of the *Encyclopedia* contains the entire text of the 1912 edition of *Wacker's Manual of the Plan of Chicago,* published by the Chicago Plan Commission for use in public schools, and this is accessible at http://www.encyclopedia.chicagohistory.org/ pages/10418.html. While *Wacker's Manual* is long out of print, copies of the 1912 and other editions can be found in libraries and used bookstores. The print version of the *Encyclopedia of Chicago,* edited (as is the electronic one) by James R. Grossman, Ann Durkin Keating, and Janice L. Reiff, was published by the University of Chicago Press in 2004.

169

The papers of Daniel H. Burnham and Edward H. Bennett are in the Ryerson and Burnham Archives of the Art Institute of Chicago. These papers pertain to the careers and lives of both men, and they contain an abundance of materials relating specifically to the *Plan,* a small portion of which are viewable in the "Interpretive Digital Essay: The *Plan of Chicago.*" A few selections from these collections also appear in this book. The Bennett papers are particularly rich in documents that reveal the day-to-day details involved in the creation and implementation of the *Plan.* While much of Burnham's correspondence relevant to creating the *Plan* is in the Bennett papers, the Burnham collection includes his handwritten draft and several of his many speeches on planning, as well as personal correspondence. The Art Institute of Chicago also owns the specially bound first copy of the *Plan* that was presented to Burnham, the originals of many of Jules Guerin's illustrations and Fernand Janin's drawings, and numerous maps and diagrams prepared for the *Plan.* The Chicago Historical Society has a few Guerin illustrations. It also possesses a large number of important papers, publications, and other materials in its Commercial Club of Chicago Collection. Its Chicago Plan Commission Lantern Slide Collection has many images prepared by the commission. The Historic Architecture and Landscape Image Collection of the Ryerson and Burnham Archives at the Art Institute also contains lantern slides used in promoting the *Plan,* a few of which are included here.

Daniel Burnham's close friend and colleague Charles Moore's admiring two-volume biography, *Daniel H. Burnham: Architect, Planner of Cities* (Boston: Houghton Mifflin, 1921), has a good selection of photographs as well as a full if uncritical account of Burnham's life. Da Capo Press reprinted this in 1968. The current standard biography of Burnham is Thomas S. Hines's excellent *Burnham of Chicago: Architect and Planner* (New York: Oxford University Press, 1974). Erik Larson's *The Devil in the White City: Murder, Magic, and Madness at the Fair that Changed America* (New York: Vintage Books, 2003) offers a detailed account of Burnham's work on the World's Columbian Exposition. Kristen Schaffer is the author of the text of *Daniel H. Burnham: Visionary Architect and Planner* (New York: Rizzoli, 2003), edited by Scott J. Tilden. This is richly illustrated with photographs by Paul Rocheleau.

Schaffer contends that Burnham's reputation has suffered unduly from both an underestimation of his creativity and personal attacks on his character. The most famous of these attacks came after Burnham's death from the pen of his contemporary Chicago architect Louis H. Sullivan in *The Autobiography of an Idea* (New York: Press of the American Institute of Architects, 1926; reprint, New York: Dover, 1956). Schaffer's outstanding introduction to the Princeton Architectural Press edition of the *Plan* is especially noteworthy in offering the best analysis of the differences between Burnham's draft and the published version edited by Moore. Schaffer's "Daniel H. Burnham: Urban Ideals and the *Plan of Chicago*" (Ph.D. diss., Cornell University, 1993) is her much more comprehensive examination of Burnham and the *Plan*.

On Bennett, see Joan E. Draper's insightful *Edward H. Bennett, Architect and City Planner, 1874–1954* (Chicago: Art Institute of Chicago, 1982). On the *Plan* itself, see the Burnham Library of Architecture's *The Plan of Chicago, 1909–1979* (Chicago: Art Institute of Chicago, 1979). Both of these are catalogs that accompanied exhibitions at the Art Institute, and the latter volume includes several valuable essays on the *Plan*. The distinguished historian Neil Harris discussed the creation of the *Plan of Chicago* in "The Planning of the *Plan*," an address delivered at the meeting of the Commercial Club on November 29, 1979, in observance of the Art Institute exhibition on the *Plan*. Roger P. Akeley's "Implementation of the 1909 *Plan of Chicago*: An Historical Account of Planning Salesmanship" (M.A. thesis, University of Tennessee, 1973) examines the *Plan*'s promotion. On the Commercial Club, see Vilas Johnson, *A History of the Commercial Club of Chicago,* published by the club in its centennial year of 1977 and including an earlier history by member John J. Glessner.

The *Plan*'s influence is only one component of the extraordinary evolution of Chicago as a built environment. The best general history of this subject, though it only goes up to the 1960s, is Harold M. Mayer and Richard C. Wade's *Chicago: Growth of a Metropolis* (Chicago:

University of Chicago Press, 1969). Equally indispensable are the two volumes that comprise Carl W. Condit's classic study of the city in the six decades following publication of the *Plan: Chicago, 1910–1929: Building, Planning, and Urban Technology* (Chicago: University of Chicago Press, 1973) and *Chicago, 1930–1970: Building, Planning, and Urban Technology* (Chicago: University of Chicago Press, 1974). Among the best more recent works on the building of the city in the nineteenth and early twentieth centuries are Daniel M. Bluestone's *Constructing Chicago* (New Haven, CT: Yale University Press, 1991); William Cronon's *Nature's Metropolis: Chicago and the Great West* (New York: W. W. Norton, 1991); and Robin F. Bachin's *Building the South Side: Urban Space and Civic Culture in Chicago, 1890–1919* (Chicago: University of Chicago Press, 2004).

For detailed studies of one element of the Chicago cityscape, see Lois Wille, *Forever Open, Clear, and Free: The Historic Struggle for Chicago's Lakefront* (Chicago: Regnery, 1972; reprint, Chicago: University of Chicago Press, 1991); John W. Stamper, *Chicago's North Michigan Avenue: Planning and Development, 1900–1930* (Chicago: University of Chicago Press, 1991); and Ross Miller, *Here's the Deal: The Buying and Selling of a Great American City* (New York: Knopf, 1996; reprint, Evanston, IL: Northwestern University Press, 2003). See also Wille's *At Home in the Loop: How Clout and Community Built Chicago's Dearborn Park* (Carbondale: Southern Illinois University Press, 1997). The Chicago Plan Commission issued regular updates on the progress of its work, which are very informative. For historical statistics on the city's life and growth in the years before and following the publication of the *Plan,* see the annual editions of the *Chicago Daily News Almanac and Yearbook.* Wesley G. Skogan's *Chicago Since 1840: A Time-Series Data Handbook* (Urbana: University of Illinois Institute of Government and Public Affairs, 1976) is also a very useful resource, as are the annual reports of different city departments. Both the Chicago Historical Society and the Municipal Reference Library at the Harold Washington Library Center own many of these reports, and the Chicago Public Library has put some of them online. For example, for the Department of Health *Summary of Vital Statistics,* see http://www.chipublib .org/004chicago/disasters/text/vitalstat/intro.html.

The scholarship on urban planning in America, let alone throughout the world, is very extensive. A good place to start is with the essays included in Donald A. Krueckeberg, ed., *Introduction to Planning History in the United States* (New Brunswick, NJ: Center for Urban Policy Research, 1983), and Daniel Schaffer, ed., *Two Centuries of American Planning* (Baltimore: Johns Hopkins University Press, 1988). Among other titles, including some outstanding recent studies, listed in chronological order, are Jane Jacobs, *The Death and Life of Great American Cities* (New York: Modern Library, 1961); Lewis Mumford, *The City in History: Its Origins, Its Transformations, and Its Prospects* (New York: Harcourt, Brace and World, 1961); Mel Scott, *American City Planning Since 1890* (Berkeley: University of California Press, 1969); Vincent Scully, *American Architecture and Urbanism* (New York: Praeger, 1969); Mark S. Foster, *From Streetcar to Superhighway: American City Planners and Urban Transportation, 1900–1940* (Philadelphia: Temple University Press, 1981); M. Christine Boyer, *Dreaming the Rational City: The Myth of American City Planning* (Cambridge, MA: MIT Press, 1983); Dolores Hayden, *Redesigning the American Dream: The Future of Housing, Work, and Family Life* (New York: W. W. Norton, 1984, 2002); Richard E. Fogelson, *Planning the Capitalist City: The Colonial Era to the 1920s* (Princeton, NJ: Princeton University Press, 1986); Peter Hall, *Cities of Tomorrow: An Intellectual History of Urban Planning and Design in the Twentieth Century* (New York: Blackwell, 1988); Stanley K. Schultz, *American Cities and City Planning, 1800–1920* (Philadelphia: Temple University Press, 1989); Jon A. Peterson, *The Birth of City Planning in the United States, 1840–1917* (Baltimore: Johns Hopkins University Press, 2003); Alison Isenberg, *Downtown America: A History of the Place and the People Who Made It* (Chicago: University of Chicago Press, 2004); and Emily Talen, *New Urbanism and American Planning: The Conflict of Cultures* (New York: Routledge, 2005). This list is selective and only suggests the full range of scholarship.

INDEX

Pages with illustrations are referred to by the page number followed by f.

Abbott, Carl, 157–59, 164
Abbott, Edith, 46–47
Acropolis, 11
Adams, Henry, xvi
Addams, Jane, xvi–xvii, 17, 45–46, 65, 78
Adler Planetarium, 141, 153, 155f
African American population, 43, 159, 164
American Academy of Arts and Sciences, 165
American Institute of Architects, 77
American Planning Association (APA), 151
Apex Building, Washington, D.C., 150
An Appeal to the Businessman, 132
Armour, Philip D., 56
Arnold, Bion J., 35, 52
Art Institute of Chicago, 25, 41f, 47, 49f, 57, 67, 77; exhibition of Plan drawings, 116; extension over Illinois Central tracks, 142–43, 144f
Ashland Avenue, 138
Association of American Architects, 62
Athens, 11
Atwood, Charles B., 26, 61f, 62
The Autobiography of an Idea (Sullivan), 19, 171
The Axis of Chicago (Bennett), 149–50

Baguio (Philippines) plan, 23
Bartlett, Adolphus, 83

Beaux Arts style, 15, 19, 163–64
Bellamy, Edward, 16–17
Bennett, Edward H., 23, 64, 69, 73f, 79f;
    Commercial Club cipher, 85, 88f;
    death, 150; promotion of the Plan, 114,
    116, 149–50; role in creation of the
    Plan, 74, 78, 85, 103–4; work for Chi-
    cago Plan Commission, 132–33, 148–
    50; zoning regulations, 132–33
Bennett, Frank, 125
Bennett, Parsons, and Frost, 148, 150
Bixby, W. H., 82
boosterism, 4, 7–10, 35, 52–53, 128
Borg-Warner Building, 63f
Breckinridge, Sophonisba, 46–47
"The Broader Aspects of City Planning"
    (Norton), 117–18
Brookfield Zoo, 147
Brooklyn Daily Eagle, 126f
Brunner, Arnold W., 23
Buckingham Fountain (Bennett, Parsons,
    and Frost), 142, 144f, 148
Building New Neighborhoods, 159
Burnham, Daniel H., xv, xvii; belief in big
    plans, 12, 154–55, 157–59, 167; City
    Beautiful movement, 14–15, 154; death,
    84, 128–29; draft manuscripts of the
    Plan, 104–10, 108f, 109f; early urban

Burnham, Daniel H. *(continued)*
planning projects, 22–23, 62, 68; grave
site, 127*f*, 129; honors and awards, 62;
iconic status, 154–55; influence on urban
planning profession, 151–52; leadership
of *Plan* committee, 66–69, 71–74, 78–
82, 84–85, 98–99, 103–10; Lincoln
Memorial project, 128; notes on Lake
Park project, 28*f*; notes on *Plan* cost es-
timates, 75*f*; personal and professional
background, 55–64; photographs, 55*f*,
59*f*, 61*f*, 73*f*; promotion of the *Plan*, 112,
116, 128; public relations skills, 30–33,
62, 67; qualities and work habits, 54, 61,
62–63; Swedenborgian faith, 32–33, 56
Burnham, Daniel H., Jr., 164
Burnham, Edwin and Elizabeth, 55
Burnham, Margaret Sherman, 57, 127*f*
Burnham and Root, 56–58, 59*f*, 94; First
Regiment Armory, 18; public and
commercial buildings, 49*f*, 57–58, 58*f*,
59*f*; residential design work, 57. *See also*
D. H. Burnham and Company
Burnham Harbor, 154
Burnham Park, 129
Burnham Plan. See *Plan of Chicago*
Busse, Fred, 77, 117, 133
Butler, Edward, 70, 73*f*, 79

Calumet Harbor, 83
Carr, Clyde M., 66, 73*f*, 77, 79, 114
Carrère, John M., 62
Carry, Edward F., 73*f*
Carter, Drake and Wight, 56
Central Area Plan of 2003, 162–63
Central Manufacturing District, 6
Century of Progress International Exposi-
tion of 1933–1934, 141, 150, 154, 155*f*
Chamberlain, Henry Barrett, 114, 116
"Chicago" (Sandburg), 52–53
Chicago 21, 162–64
"Chicago: A City of Destiny" (talk by
Goode), 5, 8
"Chicago: City of Dreams" (talk by
Mayer), 5–6, 8
Chicago: Growth of a Metropolis (Mayer and
Wade), 5–6, 171–72

"Chicago: Half Free and Fighting On"
(Steffens), 49
Chicago: Past, Present, Future (Wright), 7–8
Chicago American, 113
Chicago and South Side Rapid Transit
Company, 40
Chicago Association of Commerce, 77, 116
Chicago Board of Education, 77
Chicago Board of Trade, 7
*Chicago Can Get Fifty Million Dollars for
Nothing!*, 123
Chicago Civic Federation, 26, 49
Chicago Club (Burnham and Root), 49*f*, 57
Chicago Commercial Association, 77
Chicago Cultural Center, 47, 163*f*
Chicago Daily Chronicle, 113
Chicago Department of City Planning,
133, 161–62
Chicago Department of Planning and
Development, 133
Chicago Examiner, 116
Chicago Historical Society (Cobb), 47*f*
Chicago Inter-Ocean, 8
Chicago Manual Training School, 65
Chicago Metropolis 2020, 165–67
Chicago Metropolis 2020 organization,
165–67
Chicago Plan Commission: Bennett's work
for, 132–33, 148–50; decline in activism,
132–33; formation, 117; influence, 152–
55; later planning work, 157–61, 164;
park construction, 147; promotional
campaign, 117–29, 131–32. *See also* pro-
motion of the *Plan*
Chicago Public Library, 41*f*. *See also* Harold
M. Washington Library Center
Chicago Railway Terminal Commission,
139
Chicago Record Herald, 116
Chicago Regional Planning Association,
138, 164–65
Chicago River: bridges, 80–81; harbor
construction, 5; implementation of the
Plan, 134, 139, 140*f*; proposed diversion
of South Branch, 80; reversal of flow,
5, 14, 39; straightening project, 134, 139,
140*f*

Chicago's Greatest Issue: An Official Plan,
  122–23
Chicago Tribune, 112–14, 116, 119
Chinese population, 43, 44*f*
Circle Interchange, 138*f*
City Beautiful movement, 14–15, 67, 154;
  focus on functionality and beauty, 19,
  31; World's Columbian Exposition,
  19, 22*f*
City Club of Chicago, 159
City Hall, 41*f*, 80
City Hall–County Building, 80, 147, 162
City Homes Association, 45–46
The City in History (Mumford), 155–56
Civic Center: failure to build, 130, 138, 147;
  lantern slide of, 120–21*f*; *Plan* illustra-
  tions, 91, 104–5*f*; recommendations of
  the *Plan,* 87, 91, 94, 100*f*, 103, 147, 149–
  50. *See also* Daley Civic Center
Civic Opera House, 85
class differences, xvi; City Beautiful move-
  ment, 15; elitism of *Plan* creators, 95,
  127–28; *Plan*'s vision of urban order,
  102–3; prejudices, 14–15, 52. *See also*
  immigration; labor issues
Cleveland plan, 23, 62
Cobb, Henry Ives, 48*f*
Coliseum, 51*f*
Columbian Exposition. *See* World's
  Columbian Exposition of 1893
Columbian Fountain (MacMonnies), 22*f*
Commercial Club of Chicago, xv, xvii, 51–
  52, 64–70, 155–56; *Chicago Metropolis
  2020,* 165–67; cipher, 85, 88*f*; City
  Beautiful movement, 67; collaboration
  on the *Plan of Chicago,* 66–69, 82–83,
  104, 107, 112; Fort Sheridan, 17–18;
  Lake Park plan, 29; media attention,
  113; membership, 64–67, 71–72; ori-
  gins of the *Plan* project, 54–55; promo-
  tion and distribution of the *Plan,* 114–
  19; public contributions, 65–66;
  speakers lists, 65
Committee on the Plan of Chicago, 72–73.
  See also creation of the *Plan*
Community Conservation Board, 161

community planning and revitalization,
  157–61, 164, 167
Comprehensive Plan of Chicago of 1966, 164
Condit, Carl, 41–42
Congress Expressway, 138*f*, 152*f*
Congress Street and Parkway, 138–39, 149–
  50, 152*f*
Cook County, 165
Coughlin, "Bathhouse" John, 51, 77, 128
County Building. *See* City Hall–County
  Building
creation of the *Plan,* 71–85; collaboration
  by individuals and organizations, 54,
  64, 66–72; expenses, 74, 75*f*; first
  meeting, 72–73; funding the process,
  69–70, 73–74, 111–12; harbor planning,
  80, 82–83; information gathering, 73,
  76; lakefront planning, 73, 79, 80, 82;
  organizational support, 77; political
  lobbying, 73–74, 76–78; publication of
  the *Plan,* 74, 84–85; railroad planning,
  73, 79, 80, 83–84; roadway planning,
  73, 80–81; writing and editing process,
  103–10
Crerar Library, 87, 141–42
criticism of the *Plan,* 115*f*, 125–28, 155–59
Cronon, William, 5, 172
cultural life of Chicago: dime museums
  and cheap theaters, 50*f*; planning issues, 47–48; recommendations of the
  Plan, 87

D. H. Burnham and Company, 94; build-
  ing projects, 42–43, 47, 59–60, 63*f*; suc-
  cessor firms and projects, 148
Daley, Richard J., 156*f*, 161–64
Daley, Richard M., 162–63
Daley Civic Center, 161–62, 163
*Daniel H. Burnham: Architect, Planner of
  Cities* (Moore), 55*f*, 60*f*, 62, 104–5, 170
Dawes, Charles G., 73*f*, 125
The Death and Life of Great American Cities
  (Jacobs), 156–57
Debs, Eugene, 45
Deer Grove Forest Preserve District, 146
DeLaMater, John, 73*f*
Delano, Frederic A., 66–69, 79

demographics of Chicago: 1900–1910 census figures, 43; growth during 1800s, xv–xvi, 1–2, 7; growth of the suburbs, 159; mortality rate of 1909, 43; police arrests in 1909, 48; population density, 45–47; post–World War II racial migrations, 159; projected growth, 35; racial and ethnic composition, 43, 159; rapid transit use, 41–42; segregation, 164
Deneen, Charles, 77, 82
Development Plan for the Central Area of Chicago, 161–62
Dever, William, 133, 136
dime museums, 50*f*
dimensions of Chicago, 38–39
Donnelley, Thomas, 85
Drainage Board, 77

early plans for Chicago, 2–10; boosterism, 7–8; Central Manufacturing District, 6; Goode's views of location, 5, 8; grade elevations, 5, 6; historic precedents for, 11–18; limited nature of, 8–10; Mayer's five decisions, 5–6, 8; planning culture, 6–8; Pullman model town, 6, 15–16; transportation systems, 5–6; Union Stock Yard, 6
economic factors: commercial downtown area, 37–38; free-market economics, 3; manufacturing sector, 43–44; speculation and belief in the future, 7–8; working-class needs, 14–15
Eisenhower Expressway. *See* Congress Expressway
electric trolleys, 37*f*, 39
elevated trains. *See* rapid transit lines
Eliot, Charles W., 125
Ellsworth, James W., 26, 28*f*, 32, 67
Études sur les transformations de Paris (Hénard), 13*f*
Exposition. *See* World's Columbian Exposition of 1893

Farwell, John V., 73*f*, 82–83
Federal Center, 162
Federal Triangle, Washington, D.C., 150
Field, Marshall, 25, 26, 29, 55–56, 68

Field Museum, 153*f*, 155*f*; Commercial Club work for, 68; current location, 25; Guerin drawing, 160–61*f*; original location, 20–21*f*; proposed Grant Park location, 25; recommendations of the *Plan*, 87; Wight's Lake Park plan, 26
Fine Arts Building. *See* Museum of Science and Industry
fire of 1871. *See* Great Chicago Fire of 1871
First Regiment Armory (Burnham and Root), 18*f*
Fisher, Walter L., 87
Fitzpatrick, John, 126–27
Flatiron Building, New York (D. H. Burnham and Company), 60
Forest Preserve District, 42, 146–47
Fort Dearborn, 5, 24
Fort Sheridan, 17–18, 66
Forty-four Cities in the City of Chicago, 160
French, Daniel Chester, 22*f*
Fuller, Henry Blake, 9

Garfield Park conservatory, 42
General Committee on the Plan of Chicago, 72–73. *See also* creation of the *Plan*
George Alexander McKinlock Jr. Memorial Court, 143. *See also* Art Institute of Chicago
Gerard & Rabe Clothing Manufacturers, 44*f*
German immigration, 43
Goode, J. Paul, 5, 8
Goodman Theatre, 143
government roles in urban planning, 14
grade elevation, 5, 6*f*
Graham, Ernest R., 61*f*
Grant Park, 82, 136*f*; Buckingham Fountain, 142, 144*f*, 148; Burnham's lakefront proposals, 24–33; Guerin drawing, 160–61*f*; Illinois Central tracks, 63*f*, 142, 144*f*; implementation of the *Plan*, 141–43, 144*f*, 153–54; lakefront access, 153*f*; landfill-based expansion, 42; Olmsted Brothers' proposal, 27*f*; recommendations of the *Plan*, 130, 153
Great Chicago Fire of 1871, 4, 4*f*, 8, 47*f*, 48*f*
Great Lakes Naval Training Station, 66

Gray Wolves group in Chicago City Council, 49–51
Guerin, Jules, 84*f,* 85, 90–94, 116, 170; illustrations by, 89*f,* 92–93*f,* 96–97*f,* 158*f,* 160–61*f;* views of street life, 157, 158*f,* 160–61*f*

harbor, 5, 80, 82–83, 100*f*
Harold Washington Library Center, 162, 163*f*
Harrison, Carter, II, 49, 133–34
Harvard University, 62, 125
Haussmann, Georges-Eugène, 12
Haymarket bomb of 1886, 14, 16
Haywood, William "Big Bill," 45
Hénard, Eugène, 13
heritage of the *Plan,* 151–67; central city planning, 161–64, community planning, 157–61, 164, 167; criticism of the *Plan,* 155–59; heirs of the *Plan,* 164–67; planning profession, 151–52; quality of street life, 157–59; regional planning, 164–67
Hooker, George E., 126–27, 128
Hotel Burnham. *See* Reliance Building
housing: planning issues, 36–37, 45–47; of poorer residents, 14, 45–47; population density, 45–47; shortcomings of the *Plan,* 126–27. *See also* sanitation
How the Other Half Lives (Riis), 14
Hull-House settlement, xvi–xvii, 17*f,* 25
Hunter, Robert, 45–46
Hutchinson, Charles, 125
Hyde Park–Kenwood neighborhood, 161

Illinois and Michigan Canal, 5
Illinois Central Railroad, 24–25, 63*f,* 136*f,* 144*f*
immigration, 3–4, 7; elitist response of urban planners, 15; foreign-born percentage of Chicagoans, 43; housing, 14, 45–47; *Plan*'s vision of urban order, 102–3
implementation of the *Plan,* 130–50, 152–55; Bennett's contribution, 148–50; bond issues, 124*f,* 133; Chicago River straightening project, 134, 139, 140*f;* lakefront, 141–45; opposition to the

Plan, 115*f,* 125–28, 155–59; park systems, 141–47; political relationships, 133; railroad reorganization, 139–41; road and highway projects, 133–39; zoning regulations, 132–33
Industrial Club, 77
Industrial Workers of the World (IWW), 45
Insull, Samuel, 70
Irish immigration, 43
issues faced by Chicago's planners, 34–53; cultural life, 47–48; economic factors, 37–38; housing, 36–37, 45–47; park systems, 36, 42–43; politics, 48–51; pollution, 36; quality of life, 36; railroads, 36–37; sanitation, 36–37, 46*f;* transportation systems, 36, 37–38

Jackson Park, 8; Burnham cabin, 60*f,* 61–62; Burnham's lakefront proposals, 24, 26, 30*f,* 67, 82; implementation of the *Plan,* 141; re-landscaping, 42. *See also* World's Columbian Exposition of 1893
Jacobs, Jane, 156–57, 173
James R. Thompson Center, 162
Janin, Fernand, 85, 91, 104–5*f,* 116, 170
Jenney, William Le Baron, 56
Johnson, Elmer W., 165
John Wanamaker department store (D. H. Burnham and Company), 60
Jones, Mary Harris "Mother," 45
The Jungle (Sinclair), xvi–xvii, 44

Kenna, Mike "Hinky Dink," 51, 77, 128
Kennedy, John F., 156*f*
Kennedy Expressway, 138*f*
Kenneth Sawyer Goodman Theatre. *See* Goodman Theatre
Kingery, Robert, 164
Kingery Expressway, 164

labor issues: children, 45*f;* manufacturing, 43–44; response to the *Plan,* 126–27; strikes and violence, xvi, 14, 17–18, 44–45; union membership, 44
lakefront, 24–33, 162–63; Burnham Park, 129; Burnham's proposals for, 24, 26, 30*f,* 67, 82; creation of the *Plan,* 73, 79,

lakefront (*continued*)
    80, 82; filling, 42, 67, 141; implementation of the *Plan,* 141–45, 153–54; Lake Shore Drive, 145*f,* 146*f;* other recommendations, 162–63; parkway, 143–45; recommendations of the *Plan,* 86; Richard J. Daley's plans, 162
Lakefront Plan of Chicago, 162
Lake Park, 24–33, 67. *See also* Grant Park
Lake Shore Drive, 145*f,* 146*f,* 153*f*
Lakeside Press, 85
Lake Street Elevated Railway, 40
Land Ordinance of 1785, 5
lantern slides, 31
Lawrence, Andrew, 113
L'Enfant, Pierre-Charles, 12–13
Life on the Mississippi (Twain), 8
Lincoln Park, 42, 141, 146*f*
Link Bridge, 144–45
Little Calumet River, 39
London, 12
London Guarantee and Accident Building, 136*f*
Looking Backward (Bellamy), 16–17
the Loop Elevated Railroad, 40, 41*f*
Louis XIV, 11–12

MacMonnies, Frederick, 22*f*
MacVeagh, Franklin, 67–68, 71–72
Magnificent Mile, 135
Manila plan, 23
Marshall Field department store, 41*f,* 60, 115*f*
Mayer, Harold M., 5–6, 8, 171–72
McCormick, Edith Rockefeller, 147
McCormick, Joseph Medill, 68, 112–14
McCormick Place, 153–54
McInerney, Mike, 51
McKim, Charles F., 22–23, 62
McMillan, James, 62
media coverage of the *Plan,* 112–14, 116
Meigs Field Airport, 141, 153*f,* 154
Men Who Sell Things (Moody), 119
Merchants Club, 64–70, 164; City Beautiful movement, 67; Lake Park plan, 29; membership, 65, 71–72; merger with Commercial Club, 71; public contribu-

tions, 65–66; speakers lists, 65; support of the *Plan,* 69–70, 74–76
Merriam, Charles, 76
Metro Joe, 167
The Metropolis Plan: Choices for the Chicago Region, 166*f*
Metropolitan West Side Elevated Railroad, 40*f*
Michigan Avenue, 124*f,* 135*f,* 136*f;* bridge, 137*f,* 144, 148; implementation of the *Plan,* 134–35, 135–37*f;* Magnificent Mile, 135; *Plan* illustrations, 158*f;* promotion of the *Plan,* 113–14, 115*f;* recommendations of the *Plan,* 80–81, 106; traffic, 144
Michigan Avenue Improvement Association, 81
Midway Airport, 154
Millennium Park, 24, 148, 149*f,* 154
Monadnock Building (Burnham and Root), 57
Monroe Street, 150
Montauk Building (Burnham and Root), 59*f*
Moody, Walter L., 119–25, 131–33
Moore, Charles: biography of Burnham, 55*f,* 60*f,* 62, 104–5, 154–55, 170; writing and editing of the *Plan,* 74, 84, 103–10
Mumford, Lewis, 155–56, 157, 173
Municipal Improvement League, 26, 29
Municipal Pier, 141, 142*f,* 143*f,* 154, 162
Municipal Voters League, 49, 51
Museum of Science and Industry, 20–21*f,* 25, 26

Napoleon Bonaparte, 12
Napoleon III, 12
Native American population, 5
Navy Pier. *See* Municipal Pier
Nehemiah Day church services, 131–32
Newberry Library, 47, 48*f*
newspaper coverage of the *Plan,* 112–14, 116
New York City, xv–xvi, 60
Northerly Island, 141, 153*f,* 154, 155*f*
Northwestern Elevated Railroad, 40
Northwestern University, 62
North-West Side Monthly Bulletin, 115*f*

Norton, Charles D., 66; address to Chicago
Plan Commission, 117–18; creation of
the *Plan*, 66–69, 73*f*, 76, 79–83; implementation of the *Plan*, 148; move to
Washington, D.C., 114; promotion of
the *Plan*, 113–14; publication of the
Plan, 85

Ogden, Mahlon D., 48*f*
Ogden Avenue, 137–38
O'Hare Airport, 38, 154, 156*f*
Old Settlers, 55
Olmsted, Frederick Law, 8, 9, 101; design
for Jackson Park, 42; focus on func-
tionality and beauty, 19; World's
Columbian Exposition, 19
Olmsted, Frederick Law, Jr., 22–23
Olmsted Brothers Landscape Architects,
25, 27*f*
opposition to the *Plan*, 115*f*, 125–28, 155–59
Orchestra Hall (D. H. Burnham and Com-
pany), 47, 60, 63*f*
Outer Belt Commission, 42, 145–46

Palace of Fine Arts, 20–21*f*
Palmer, Bertha and Potter, 145*f*
Panic of 1837, 7–8
Paris, 11–12, 13*f*, 34, 95, 130
parks, 5, 8, 42–43, 87, 145–47, 159; Brook-
field Zoo, 147; expansion by landfill,
42, 67; Forest Preserve District, 146–
47; implementation of the *Plan*, 141–
47; planning issues, 36, 42–43; recom-
mendations of the *Plan*, 86–87, 100*f*,
101, 130; recreation and playground
facilities, 24, 25, 42–43, 66, 102. *See also*
Grant Park; lakefront of Chicago
Pennsylvania Railroad, 140
Pericles, 11
Perkins, Dwight H., 25
Pickett, M. B., 61*f*
Pine Street, 81, 135. *See also* Michigan
Avenue
planning profession, 151–52
Planning the Region of Chicago (Burnham Jr.
and Kingery), 164–65
Plan of Chicago, xv, 19, 88*f*; authorship and

revisions, 103–10; Axis of Chicago,
138–39, 149–50, 152; Burnham's ceremonial copy, 116–17; condensed versions, 122–25; contents, 86–110; cover,
85, 88*f*; "heart" metaphor, 95–98, 162;
iconic status, 154–55; illustrations and
photographs, 34, 73*f*, 84–85, 89*f*, 90–
94, 96–97*f*, 104*f*, 157–59, 166*f*; legal aspects, 87; map, 3*f*; physical characteris-
tics of the book, 85, 87–91, 11–12;
Princeton Architectural Press facsimile
edition, 104, 169; publication, 2, 85;
quality of street life, 157–61; recommendations, 86–87, 99–103, 105–6, 130,
147, 152–55; sanitary reform, 99–101;
title page, 90*f*; view of capitalism, 101;
vision of urban experience, 94–98,
102–3
political life of Chicago: corruption and
efforts at reform, 49–52; endorsements
of the *Plan*, 117–19; local power, 48–49,
77; planning issues, 48–51. *See also* implementation of the *Plan*
pollution, xvi, 36, 37*f*
population: expulsion of Native Americans, 5; growth in 1800s and early
1900s, xv–xvi, 1–2, 7; immigration, 3–
4, 7; mobility, 4; post World War II
racial migrations, 159; segregation, 164
Post Office. *See* United States Post Office
Powers, Johnny, 51
Prairie Avenue neighborhood, 18
press coverage of the *Plan*, 112–14, 116
promotion of the *Plan*, 111–29, 131–32,
149–50; film, 125; fund-raising, 119;
lectures and slide shows, 120–21*f*, 122,
170; Nehemiah Day church services,
131–32; newspaper and magazine coverage, 112–14, 125–28; opposition, 115*f*,
125–28; political endorsements, 117–19;
publications, 122–25; rallies, 124*f*; release events, 114–16; school edition,
124–25, 126*f*, 132
Public article, 127–28
Publication Committee, 114–19
publicity. *See* promotion of the *Plan*
Public Works Administration, 145

Pullman, George, 15, 26, 56
Pullman model town, 6, 15–16, 16*f*
Pullman strike of 1894, 14, 16

railroads, xvi, 5, 63*f*; creation of the *Plan,*
    73, 79, 80, 83–84; freight terminals, 140;
    implementation of the *Plan,* 139–41;
    planning issues, 36–37; recommenda-
    tions of the *Plan,* 86, 100*f*
Railway Exchange Building (D. H. Burn-
    ham and Company), 60, 62, 63*f*; D. H.
    Burnham and Company offices, 73*f*,
    74; rooftop drafting rooms, 74, 75*f*, 77
Rand-McNally Building (Burnham and
    Root), 57
rapid transit lines, 40–42
Real Estate Board, 77
recommendations of the *Plan. See Plan of
    Chicago*
reform efforts, xvi–xvii, 165; City Beautiful
    movement, 14–15, 19, 22*f*, 31, 67, 154;
    Hull-House settlement, 17, 25; immi-
    grant housing, 14; Progressivism, 12,
    147; Pullman model town, 6, 15–16
regional planning, 138, 164–67
Reliance Building (D. H. Burnham and
    Company), 59–60
the *Republic* statue (French), 22*f*
Richard J. Daley Civic Center, 161–62, 163
Riis, Jacob, 14, 65
Riverside suburb, 8
roads and boulevards, 5; creation of the
    Plan, 73, 80–81; funding, 124*f*, 145;
    highway development, 138; implemen-
    tation of the *Plan,* 133–39; recommen-
    dations of the *Plan,* 86–87, 105–6; traf-
    fic congestion, 123*f*
Robinson, Theodore W., 73*f*, 117–18
Rome, 11
Rookery Building (Burnham and Root),
    57, 58*f*, 59*f*
Roosevelt Road, 153*f*. *See also* Twelfth
    Street improvement
Root, John Wellborn, 56–58, 59*f*
Rush Street Bridge, 135
Ryan Expressway, 138*f*

Saint-Gaudens, Augustus, 22–23, 62
Sandburg, Carl, 52–53
San Francisco plan, 23, 62, 68
Sanitary Canal, 39, 42
Sanitary District of Chicago, 14, 65, 157
sanitation, xvi, 39, 159; planning issues, 36–
    37, 46*f*; *Plan* recommendations, 99–101
Santa Fe Building (D. H. Burnham and
    Company), 60, 63*f*
Schaffer, Kristen, 104–6, 170–71
Schuyler, Montgomery, 19
Scott, John W., 73*f*, 112–14, 116
Scully, Thomas F., 134
Second Regiment Armory, 66
segregation, 164
Seymour, H. W., 113
The Shame of the Cities (Steffens), 49
Shedd, John G., 73*f*, 125, 153
Shedd Aquarium, 141, 148, 152–53, 155*f*
Shepley, Rutan, and Coolidge, 49*f*
Sheridan Road, 138
Sherman, John B., 32, 43, 57
Sherman home (Burnham and Root), 57
Sherman Park, 42–43
Simpson, James, 132–33
Sinclair, Upton, xvi–xvii, 44
Skokie Valley, 146
Snow, Bernard W., 118–19
Soldier Field, 141, 152, 153*f*, 155*f*
*An S–O–S to the Public Spirited Citizens of
    Chicago,* 132
South Park Commission, 26, 29, 32, 42, 157
South Shore Drive and Waterway, 30*f*
Special Park Commission, 25, 36, 42, 145–
    46, 157
Sprague, A. A., II, 136–37
State of Illinois Center. *See* James R.
    Thompson Center
State Street Mall, 162
Steevens, George Warrington, 38
Steffens, Lincoln, 49
stockyard strikes of 1902 and 1904, 44–45
Straus Building, 63*f*
Street, Julian, 38
suburban growth, 159
Sullivan, Louis, 19, 171

Survey article, 126
Swift, George B., 26

Taft, William Howard, 60, 116, 128
A Tale of One City (film), 125
Taylor, Eugene, 122, 132–33
teamsters strike of 1905, 44–45
telephone service, 39
The Tenement Conditions in Chicago (City
    Homes Association), 45–46
Thomas, Theodore, 60*f*
Thompson, William Hale "Big Bill," 51,
    124*f*, 133, 135*f*
Thorne, Charles H., 73*f*
tourists' accounts, 38
traffic circles, 13*f*
transportation: airports, 141, 154, 156*f*; early
    planning, 5–6; implementation of the
    Plan, 140–41; the Loop, 40, 41*f*; planning
    issues, 36, 37–38; rapid transit lines, 40–
    42; recommendations of the *Plan*, 86–
    87, 100*f*; shortcomings of the *Plan*,
    126–27; streetcars and trolleys, 37*f*, 39;
    streets and bridges, 39; subway system,
    140–41, 159; traffic circles, 13*f*; traffic
    congestion, 37*f*, 37–38. *See also* railroads
Tribune Tower, 135, 136–37*f*
Tuttle, Emerson B., 73*f*
Twain, Mark, 8
Twelfth Street improvement, 133–34. *See*
    also Roosevelt Road
Twenty Years at Hull-House (Addams), xvi–
    xvii

Union Elevated Railroad, 40
Union League Club, 66
Union Station, Chicago, 139, 148
Union Station, Washington, D.C. (D. H.
    Burnham and Company), 60
Union Stock Yard, 6, 57
United States Post Office, 147–48, 150, 152*f*
University Club, 66
University of Chicago, 161
University of Illinois at Chicago, 138*f*, 162
U.S. Army Corps of Engineers, 82
U.S. Commission of Fine Arts, 128

Wacker, Charles H., 137; Chicago Plan
    Commission, 117, 118*f*, 119, 122, 124*f*,
    132–33, 146, 147; creation of the *Plan*,
    73*f*; promotion of the *Plan*, 114–25
Wacker Drive, 130, 134, 136–37
Wacker's Manual of the Plan of Chicago
    (Moody), 123–25, 132, 167, 169
Wade, Richard C., 5, 171–72
Wanamaker department store. *See* John
    Wanamaker department store
Ward, A. Montgomery, 24–26, 141–42
Washington, Booker T., 65
Washington, D.C., 12–13; Federal Triangle
    plan, 150; Lincoln Memorial plan, 128;
    Mall plan, 22–23, 62, 68, 85
Washington, George, 12
Washington Park, 8
waterworks, 5, 39, 159
Western Avenue, 138
Western Society of Engineers, 77
What of the City? (Moody), 119–22, 135*f*
Wight, Peter B., 26
William Weil's Chicago Band, 124*f*
Wilmette Harbor, 39
Wilson, Walter H., 67–70, 113, 117
With the Procession (Fuller), 9
Wobblies (IWW), 45
Woodlawn Planning Committee, 160
World's Columbian Exposition of 1893,
    xvi, 8, 19, 20–21*f*, 22*f*; Court of Honor,
    19, 20–21*f*, 22*f*, 61*f*; cultural and intel-
    lectual gatherings, 49*f*; Field Museum,
    20–21*f*, 25; Museum of Science and In-
    dustry, 20–21*f*, 25; planning of, 58, 65;
    Wooded Island cabin, 60*f*, 61–62
World's Fair of 1933–1934. *See* Century of
    Progress International Exposition of
    1933–34
World War I, 131
World War II, 159
Wren, Christopher, 12
Wright, John S., 7–8, 10
Wrigley Building, 135, 136*f*

Yale University, 62